75 STRONG

The 75 Day Challenge to Build a Stronger You

CARLOS GRIDER

Buffalo Posting Publishing

Copyright © 2021 Carlos Grider

All rights reserved. No part of this publication may be reproduced, distributed, or transmitted by any means, including photocopying, recording, or other electronic or mechanical methods without the prior written permission of the publisher, except in the case of brief quotations embodied in critical reviews and certain other noncommercial uses permitted by copyright law. For permission requests, contact the publisher, addressed "Attention: Permissions Coordinator"

ISBN: 9798754315570 (Paperback)
ASIN: B09KDL4QZ8 (Paperback)

Cover design by: Carlos Grider
Printed in the United States of America

WANT A FREE 15 MINUTE VIDEO OVERVIEW OF THE 75 STRONG CHALLENGE?

75 Strong is a great read, but at 150 pages I realize it will take the average person a few days to read it.

I believe the strategies container in this book and this program are so powerful, I want you to know about them, NOW!

So, I want to give you a 15 minute overview, on video, covering everything in this book, free!

Additionally, I want to give you a free 75 Strong checklist and a free 75 day journal, and one other tool to craft a stronger you and a better life.

(A $49 Value - yours Free!)

To get your bonuses, visit https://abrotherabroad.com/get-75-strong-freebies

CONTENTS

- Preface
- Intro: The Pandemic, Isolation, Loss of Structure, and Building New Routines
- Chapter 1: The Other 75 Day Challenges - The Inspiration for the 75 Strong Challenge
- Chapter 2: Introducing the 75 Strong Challenge: Building 10 Essential Habits for a Stronger Existence In 75 Days
- Chapter 3: 8 Tenets for the 75 Strong Program...and Life: The Guiding Spirit of 75 Strong
- Chapter 4: More Tips for a Successful and Worthwhile Challenge
- Chapter 5: The 10 Daily Tasks In Depth
  - **1. Be Thankful:** List 20 Things You Are Thankful For
  - **2. Appreciate Yourself:** List 20 Things You Admire About Yourself
  - **3. Be Still:** Sit Quietly or Meditate for 15 Minutes
  - **4. Move and Mobilize:** Exercise or Stretch
  - **5. Eat Healthily**: Limit sugar and refined carbohydrates and add nutrient dense foods
  - **6. Skip Alcohol**
  - **7. Read or Listen to a Book** for 15 Minutes
  - **8. Learn a New Concept or Skill** for 15 Minutes
  - **9. Do Something You're Passionate About** for 15

Minutes
- **10. Record the Process and Acknowledge Your Efforts**
- Chapter 6: Military Tough: Elite Military Training as a Model for a Worthwhile 75 Day Challenge
- Chapter 7: What Next: Beyond the 75 Strong Challenge

PREFACE

LIFE WAS GOOD. THEN, THE PANDEMIC STARTED

When the pandemic started, I was still on the move wandering Southeast Asia, travel writing to my heart's contentment. I spent my time bouncing between islands, climbing volcanoes, and surfing my way around Southeast Asia. My life was filled with fulfilling activities and positive habits. Surfing, exercising, hiking and doing anything else I loved was normal and nearly essential in my daily routine. My routine naturally exposed me to the new adventures, cultural experiences, and practical education experiences I needed on a daily basis.

At the start of 2020, that flow and rhythm halted to a stop. My accidental but meaningful "system" of exploration and very unconventional yet fulfilling travel and exploration all but ceased as I settled into a life of isolation while the world made compromises to stave off the impending pandemic at this pivotal moment. Unfortunately, during the shift, I allowed external factors to change my perception of my adopted home of Bali from a nest of discovery into a paralyzing cocoon as my positive habits and routines gradually faded from my life and the staleness of isolation set in.

Two hour-long surf sessions gave way to 10-minute walks through fields of cows just to get sunlight. Exploring local markets and practicing Indonesian gave way to binging Netflix and wasting time scrolling on social media. Thoughts of positivity and hopeful plans for the future gave way to pessimism, ungratefulness, and worry as confusion about the future crept in. The habits in my life of discovery slowly disintegrated, and with it, the mechanisms that I relied on to support my routines that, normally, kept me healthy, happy and productive. There was no longer a beach to visit encouraging me to experience nature and move my body. No coworking space to cut out distractions and force focus on new ideas and writing. No foreign language to navigate, to encourage me to push myself mentally.

In quarantine and isolation, I had only myself and the habits I was disciplined enough to maintain.

Fast forward months ahead. I was still in isolation. I was a little less fit. I was a little less productive. I was a little less positive. I felt a little less lively.

There are a lot of factors I could *attempt* to blame this loss on, but, the only thing truly responsible for this change, this loss of positive structure and forward movement in life, was me. I allowed myself to lose my foundational habits. I relied too much on the external situation and external elements to maintain positive flow in my life.

I didn't intentionally maintain the routine tasks that mattered to my long-term goals and that were necessary to be the person I continually wanted to be.

That was my mistake. That was the only mistake that mattered.

Through this mistake, of letting my own structure slip, I wasted the *opportunity* of months in isolation. Months I could have spent building the body of my dreams through home workouts and healthy eating. Months that I could have spent learning new skills to build the business I'd always wanted. Months that I could have used reconnecting with friends and loved ones daily. Months during which I could have started building *that thing* I've been dreaming about for years.

And I imagine, if you're reading this, you felt the same way.

You might not feel that missed opportunity from quarantine and isolation. Maybe you feel the missed opportunities that can come from investing too much energy and time in a job that isn't your calling. Maybe you allowed yourself to become paralyzed in an unsuitable relationship. Maybe you simply didn't do what was necessary to seize the opportunity of life that was is in front of you at some point.

Luckily for you and me, we can't go back in time and try to change the past – literally or figuratively, obsessing in our minds – and we don't have to. We don't have to worry about that potential regret filled mental and emotional burden. However, we can shape the future into whatever we want it to be – no time machine necessary.

MY WAKEUP CALL

One day, I broke the rules of isolation and snuck to the beach with my surfboard, and paddled through the breaking waves for a session of surfing, the first in months. It was *miserable*! Not because of the water temperature, or the violence of the waves, or even the board, but because of me. I'd let myself and my standards slip during isolation. In turn, the ability to surf, and enjoy it, was what I sacrificed as a result. I'd allowed myself to get out of shape. I felt weak.

Surfing is something I love. Something I'm passionate about. In spite of that, I let the routines of fitness and healthy eating in my life slip so much that the loss negatively affected how well I could enjoy my passion. Paddling against the waves for 10 minutes left me winded, frustrated, and getting nowhere. That realization made me angry.

After a very short and embarrassing session on the waves, I let the ocean push me back to shore.

I sat there on the beach with my surfboard, the sunshine, and not a soul around. I reflected for a good 30 minutes. The realizations flooded over me like the waves crashing on that shore.

I realized that, for the past few months, I had allowed everything around me to dictate which parts of me I maintained and which parts of me I allowed myself to lose.

My degraded surfing skills were likely the tip of the iceberg of potential that faded with the self-discipline I lost and the personal maintenance routines that faded. If I had dug deeper, how much opportunity and productivity would I realize had been sacrificed with the loss of the positive habits and structure in my life?

Most importantly, I realized there was no reason to dwell. As that epic movie about isolation, confinement, and mental prisons, Shawshank Redemption, stated, "get busy living or get busy dying."

I left the beach and got to it. I wrote out a fitness plan specifically for isolation and working out at home. I wrote eating guidelines to fuel the progress and strength I wanted back and to replace eating habits that weighted me down and reduced my physical potential. I created an education plan focused on learning that would lead to my goals. And so many more things. Ultimately, I listed the tasks that I needed in order to return to the old me, except a better version.

The remainder of isolation wouldn't be a prison, it would be finishing school.

Fast forward one month. I had dropped pounds and felt more energetic. My surfing was back to normal, sneaking out at sunrise to wander the waves alone. I had written a book and sold new work for my business. I was waking up earlier and with more energy. I felt happier, healthier, and more alive than ever. These changes all happened because of my intentional and deliberate action to rebuild positive routines in my life aligned with the person I wanted to be and was committed to being.

I realized that having routines that could be maintained indefinitely and had positive outcomes no matter the external circumstances were the keys to continuing success.

As I saw positive results, I continued to add more tasks and more routines, creating a positive feedback loop. The more work I put in, the better I felt, the more motivated I felt, the more committed I became to the work, and the more results I saw, which motivated me more.

Amidst all this, one day it hit me – I hadn't been this fit or productive since my days in the Marine Corps. I had this "tool kit" all along as a means to condition myself for my objective - live an enjoyable, fulfilling, and productive life, I had just forgotten about it.

I'd taken it for granted. Now, I remembered. I had that capability again, and I was using it to become the best version of myself I'd ever been.

Losing those foundational habits was like giving away my power. By doing so, I unintentionally compromised being physically, mentally, and emotionally ready for anything. That compromise put me at risk of losing the opportunities that frequently arise to make the most of life.

I realized, it takes intention to maintain structure and foundation in our lives. It takes intention to maintain the strength – mental and physical – that we need to overcome obstacles and achieve our goals. Especially when the world around us disintegrates.

I then audited my daily life. I took stock of the high value, beneficial habits and routines I let slip. I acknowledged the strengths I value but let gradually fade away. I acknowledged the uncharacteristic, lackadaisical state I let myself slip into.

I decided to identify and double down on the positive habits I wanted to keep. I decided through thick and thin I would maintain that structure and, consequently, my quality of life no matter what the world would throw at me.

Then, I got moving.

ENTER: THE NEW NORMAL

Mornings started with a routine. Instead of honing in on what was wrong, I focused on the amazing gifts and opportunities that surrounded me. Instead of getting down on myself for wasted time, I identified what I was doing right and made a plan to repeat it. I exercised. I meditated. I got in gear.

Quarantine and isolation were no longer paralyzing prisons. They were opportunities.

STUMBLING ON THE POPULAR 75 DAY CHALLENGES

Months later, after I regained my routines and habits, a friend posted on social media about one of the many 75 day challenges. Essentially, these challenges consisted of committing to 75 days straight of working out daily (sometimes twice daily), dieting, skipping drinking, and a few other good habits.

I loved the idea.

Committing to 75 days of life-improving habits is a no-brainer opportunity. Why *wouldn't* anyone do it?

So, I started a 75 day challenge.

By day three, three important things hit me.

1) I had unintentionally been doing the challenge on a Monday through Friday basis for months. Also, the challenge was structured like daily routines in combat deployments and military courses, so, the challenge was nothing new.

2) There was a lot of room for improvement in the challenge I chose. There were potential tweaks that could make it safer and healthier. There was also opportunity to add in an "emotional hygiene" element, and address the all too often neglected problem of mental health that reared its ugly head during isolation and the dark parts of our lives.

3) The challenges seemed to lack the long-term benefits and focus on self-development that was a clear opportunity in the challenge. The most popular 75 day challenge seemed to be focused on finishing and sharing the results. Done. That's it. However, the most effective training and opportunities to be "challenged" in life condition us in positive ways that become instinctive and remain paying dividends indefinitely. There was an opportunity to make the challenge less about finishing and bragging rights, and more about beneficial changes that lasted beyond day 75 – healthy, long term habits.

The other 75 day challenges were a good start, a reminder of a system I used before. Not necessarily to become "tough," but to become and stay an effective Marine, and human being.

Despite the popular challenge's creation starting with great intentions, there was room to improve. We could easily make the achievements, and results, stick long term. We could aim to program ourselves using daily "tasks" that ultimately become sustainable habits. This is similar to elite military training - programming skillsets and toolsets that border on being autonomic.

There was also room to make this development holistic. We could condition not just the body or lightly condition the mind but add strength and grit to our whole being, strengthening ourselves physically, mentally, and emotionally.

Though the challenge needed to be reshaped, it still added a whole new layer of intentionality to the new "system" I already had in place. It wasn't perfect, just like my approach of adding new tasks and habits daily wasn't, but it was still a great start.

By combining one of the popular 75 day challenges' approach with the time-tested approach to programming that I experienced in the Marine Corps, and a lot of evidence from clinical research studies, we would have a perfect approach to building new, positive habits for the long term.

On Day 3 of my 75 day challenge (one of the earlier, popular 75 day challenges), I tweaked, shifted, and scribbled something that focused on creating a stronger me in the long term. The 75 Strong program was born.

THE BIRTH OF THE 75 STRONG PROGRAM

The book you are about to read is about the 75 Strong challenge, an intentional program designed to ingrain positive, empowering habits in 75 days. Each habit will undoubtedly improve the quality of your life and empower you to accomplish goals and climb mountains that you couldn't (or thought you couldn't) before.

The foundation of the program consists of the following 10 daily "tasks" that we'll call the "daily 10" and complete at least 9 of every 10 days.

1. **Be Thankful:** List 20 things you're thankful for, written or aloud

2. **Self-Appreciation:** List 20 things you appreciate about yourself, written or aloud

3. **Be Still:** Sit in silence and stillness for 15 minutes

4. **Move and Mobilize:** Workout for two days, then take one day to recover and stretch, then repeat

5. **Eat Healthily**

- Eat meat and vegetables, nuts and seeds, some fruit, , no processed sugar, minimal refined carbs, low starch
- Consider intermittent fasting by eating within an 8 to 12 hour window daily (talk to your physician before taking on this task)

6. **Skip alcohol** completely

7. **Read or listen to a book** for 15 minutes, fiction or non-fiction

8. **Learn a new concept or skill** for 15 minutes

9. **Express a passion** for 15 minutes

10. **Record the process** daily in a checklist and journal your thoughts and realizations

These "Daily 10" tasks you'll complete (soon to be habits) are all potential habits and ideas that I learned from leaders and guides I respected and saw reasons to emulate. I learned these habits from battle hardened warriors, monks, professors, and more. I tried each habit on for size, and saw clear benefits from each, so much that I decided to continue each habit in my daily life, indefinitely. Now I am recommending them to you.

We will get into the science later, but performing each of these tasks 9 out of every 10 days for 75 days exceeds the average threshold for making an action a habit. According to the research, if you can hit 66 repetitions, you'll have a new positive, empowering habit, or reprogram an undesirable habit.

HOW THIS PROGRAM WORKS

In this program, we have identified the small actions that, if conditioned to the point of habit and repeated indefinitely (and each action can definitely be repeated indefinitely), act as tools for maintaining and improving your quality of life, with minimal mental effort in the long term.

By encouraging you to perform difficult but beneficial tasks over a long period, this program additionally trains "grit", a valuable character trait for resilience, strength, and productivity in our daily lives.

Grit, the perseverance of effort in pursuit of a long-term goal, is one of the single most important ingredients to being successful. This is because, no matter what life throws at you, having the ability to continue the positive actions and underlying routines through pain, heartache, despair, and confusion will get you through *anything*. By training the muscles, physical and mental, to just "do" when something needs to be done in order to improve your life and move closer to an objective, we are increasing your grit, and your toughness, by increasing your physical, mental, and emotional strength as well as your foundations over the next 75 days. 75 days to a stronger you.

WHY SHOULD YOU CARE?

You should care because no matter who you are these "Daily 10" tasks are potential tools for creating a better life and a more effective approach to daily life.

Being intentionally appreciative of what you have around you *will* lead to having more of what you appreciate and ultimately a better quality of life.

Showing yourself more appreciation for your existing greatness *will* lead to positive feelings of self-confidence and contentment and an ultimately stronger you.

Using and moving your body *will* lead to a stronger, more capable body, a stronger you, and a better life.

Drinking less alcohol *will* improve how your body functions, your clarity of mind, and your quality of life.

And completing this challenge will ingrain all of these positive actions into your life as autonomic routines.

You should care and make the attempt because you can't reasonably argue that any of these actions aren't worth doing. You can't argue that each of these actions won't improve your life.

Repeating these actions for 75 days *will* make them habits that will lead to a better life or at the very least reprogram your relationship with your existing detrimental habits.

Doing this program, 75 strong, takes the complexity out of programming functional, positive daily actions.

75 Strong doesn't make adding these habits easy. However, it does make it doable.

WHY 75 DAYS?

Research has shown, it takes 66 days, on average, to build a habit. If you accomplish every task 9 of every 10 days then by day 75 you will hit 67 repetitions. This is just enough to make that daily task a new habit – an autonomic positive behavior in your life.

We'll get into the science later, but understand that 75 days of attempts + room for human error = a new habit.

WHY I WROTE THIS BOOK

I decided to write this book because *this* – a structured approach to building mentally and physically strong human beings - is something that needs to be shared, given the recent events and our current situations globally and individually.

I wrote this book because you can't go wrong by building more grit – the ability to rise against challenges and persevere in the long term – or have a system for keeping positive momentum when life gets rough. Not everyone can go to Marine Boot Camp, or even needs to. However, everyone can apply this 75 day program, anywhere. Everyone can, with discipline and diligence, build a solid level of productivity, efficiency, fulfillment, and intentionality into their lives, by reprogramming a foundation of positive habits.

In some way, shape, or form, the "Daily 10" tasks have gotten me through war, through jobs I hated, and through the most confusing times in life. In the same moment, these 10 tasks have empowered me with the confidence, ability, and toolset to craft the life I've always wanted.

These habits weren't my idea. They were given to me. It is only right that I pay it forward by sharing these ideas with anyone who has the drive to build them into their own life. That is why I've written this book.

I wish I'd found these ten daily practices when I was 18 years old, leaving home without a road map. It's too late for that. That time has passed, no sense regretting it.

However, my appreciation that I have them now is stronger than that wish.

What I can do is share them with "18-year-old someone else." What I can do is share the 75 Strong approach with someone else who lost their path in isolation, in a fading relationship, or in a job that didn't suit them.

I am writing this to hand you a tool kit to get back to the best of you, the strongest of you.

Having the ability to condition ourselves with positive habits that feel effortless and are unaffected by external stressors is universally positive.

The better you are, the better the world we live in becomes. *That* is why I'm writing this.

75 days. You've got this. Let's get after it. I'll see you on the other side.

- C

INTRODUCTION TO THE 75 STRONG PROGRAM

"The positive habits in life need to be routine and automatized. They must be turned into regular and reliable habits, so they lose complexity and gain predictability and simplicity."

- From the book "12 Rules for Life" by Jordan Peterson

This excellent piece of advice highlights the important opportunity to make every action in our 75 day challenge a positive new habit or routine that we maintain and benefit from in the long term.

This book, 75 Strong, leverages the training, experience, and knowledge I've received from countless teachers and distilled into a 75-day plan for programming high benefit habits into your life. Even better, you can continue each habit indefinitely and all of them will benefit you more and more as you continue to apply them.

My experiences and lessons from meditation studies at a monastery, advanced military training, six combat deployments, 50+ countries traveled, countless cultures I have explored and experienced, and – most importantly – listening to the wisdom of the many teachers I've been lucky to be taught by form the foundation of this book.

The goal of this book, 75 Strong, is to ingrain 10 specific new positive habits into your life over the next 75 days that will stick with you (and improve your life) indefinitely.

If you want to get after it and get to results quickly, jump right to chapter 2, read the list of the "Daily 10" tasks and how to do them, and start doing them today. Then, as you have the time, read the rest of the book.

If you want the full experience to understand why the Daily 10 tasks will be so empowering in your life and want to understand why the 75 Strong approach is better than other options, then start here and read through the first chapter. Then, when you're convinced, start your Daily 10 and get after it.

CHAPTER 1: THE INSPIRATION FOR 75 STRONG

Back in 2019, someone had a great idea and shared that idea with the world. For 75 days straight complete a set of tasks to "build toughness." These tasks included the following:

1. Workout twice a day for at least 45 minutes
2. Follow a diet
3. Drink 4 liters of water per day
4. Read 10 pages of non-fiction per day
5. No alcohol
6. Take a progress photo

Simple as that. Complete every single one of these actions for 75 days straight. If you miss 1 day, you restart back at day 1.

The aim of this challenge was to build mental toughness, and it spread in popularity like wildfire.

Any attempt to maintain 75 days straight of *any* positive action is commendable. However, as great as the originator's intentions were, there is always room for improvement – even in the original 75 day challenges.

Conversations quickly began as to whether the challenge was safe and worth the 75-day investment.

WHETHER THE ORIGINAL 75 DAY CHALLENGE IS RISKY *FOR YOU* DEPENDS ON HOW YOU APPROACH THE CHALLENGE.

If you're assessing whether anything is healthy long term then ask yourself, "If I continued these tasks every day, indefinitely, would the results be positive in the long term?"

The answer to that question is your answer overall.

If the answer is yes, if you continued doing those tasks every day, forever, and the results would still be positive, you're building positive habits and long-term change that's right for you. That's great. Go for it.

If the answer is "no," there may be some risks to acknowledge and address.

From the perspective of a former fitness trainer and Crossfit trainer with years of experience, I would not recommend two workouts a day for most people. Most bodies can't stand up to, or benefit in the long term, from that kind of program. I definitely would not recommend two workouts a day to anyone who hasn't been continuously active. I absolutely would not recommend exercising for 75 days straight if our goal is improvement, not destruction.

From the perspective of a former Marine who has been through intense military training adding up to years in total, if we're going to invest 75 days into becoming stronger and better, there is a lot more we can accomplish in those 75 days.

But the real question is why do you want to do the challenge? What are you hoping to gain from this 75 day commitment?

WHETHER THE ORIGINAL 75 DAY CHALLENGE WOULD BE WORTHWHILE FOR YOU DEPENDS ON WHAT YOU HOPE TO GAIN FROM YOUR COMMITMENT.

Assessing whether the original 75 day challenge is for you doesn't just depend on how it affects you now, it also depends on what you want to achieve

When taking on "challenges" like these, you have to choose between two types of goals.

Are you doing the challenge just to say you did something tough? Or to prove something to yourself?

Or, are you doing this challenge to create sustainable positive results?

If you simply want to do something hard, and you're not looking for sustained results, the original 75 day challenge may be fine for you as is.

However, if your goal is to build lasting positive change and a system to maintain it, we can accomplish much more in line with your goals in our 75 days.

If you don't want to just get fit, but want to stay fit, and not just lose weight, but keep it off, we can take a better approach to your goals. If you ultimately want positive *habits*, like reading more or drinking alcohol less, we can do more in 75 days. We can achieve lasting positive change with minimal risk.

Suppose we approach the 75 days not as a "test", but as a catalyst to reprogram bad routines in daily life and build in new, healthy, empowering habits and personal improvements. Then this challenge has the potential to be universally beneficial to anyone. *That* is 75 Strong.

CONCERNS WITH THE POPULAR 75 DAY CHALLENGES

Though the other popular 75 day challenges are good starting points for sparking change in one's life, there are a few points of concern. The focus and frequency of some tasks potentially make the challenges risky for some. However, these potential trouble points are opportunities we can improve on to create a more worthwhile 75 day program.

The challenge doesn't fully use the "investment" of 75 days – we can achieve more.

The tasks and respective schedule of the tasks in the original 75 day challenge aren't sustainable indefinitely. Most of the "tasks" will die off in most people's routines after the 75 days.

The structure and check in points of the original 75 day challenge feeds the idea that "instantly observable progress" is what matters. In reality, the process and diligence are actually what matter most.

The list of tasks misses an opportunity for mental and emotional hygiene and recovery.

Some of the other challenges require you to restart at day one if you miss a single day. In reality, forward progress matters more than perfection.

Now, let's dig into each of the opportunities for improvement.

THE ORIGINAL CHALLENGE DOESN'T MAXIMIZE THE LONG-TERM RESULTS WE COULD GAIN FROM SUCH A LARGE "INVESTMENT" OF 75 DAYS

The original 75 day challenge was structured simply as that: a challenge. A test. A marathon wherein the finish line is where things end.

The original 75 day challenge is a *test* intended to be completed. This isn't necessarily bad – tests carry value in themselves as assessment and development tools. However, tests are not necessarily suited to every objective.

By nature, the primary goal of challenges is completion. Just like a race. Just like any task. Upon completion, we return to our normal lives with a badge of honor that we "finished" the challenge and data that *could* guide toward improvement if we take the next steps.

But growth should never be complete. The process of development should never be complete. The results of such an investment shouldn't end.

Seventy-five days is a significant investment. If we are going to dedicate 75 days to anything, we should see significant and lasting benefits.

An example of a challenge that was a true investment for me was Marine Corps Boot Camp. Marine Corps Boot Camp was only 13 weeks. Twenty years later, the habits and standards I internalized in that experience still drive me to success and are still constantly improving my life today. The standards of being loyal, never quitting, acting to influence what you control and dismissing what you cannot are lessons and standards I picked up then that have stayed with me. Our 75 days should be no different in producing results, and should be just as beneficial long term.

If you invest 75 days, ensure that investment will pay dividends long after the challenge ends.

The tasks in the original 75 day challenge aren't sustainable indefinitely. Most of the "tasks" will die off in our routines after 75 days

These tasks – reading daily, exercising daily, eating healthily – definitely have benefits in the short term. But these actions would be most beneficial in the long term if they were continued for the rest of our lives. For these actions to become habits, continued indefinitely, they need to be sustainable.

We need to be able to do these actions week after week, year after year, with no detriment to our health and continued (ideally increasing) benefit.

Two workouts a day, every day, isn't sustainable or advisable for most people. Adequate time for recovery is necessary for improvement. As such, the two workouts a day approach doesn't contribute to a healthy habit of fitness in the long term.

Strenuous workouts drive strength increases, cardiovascular improvement, health benefits, and longevity benefits. But adequate recovery time is required for the full process of recovery and improvement to take place. The tissue damage and spikes in positive hormones that result help your body rebuild itself stronger as you "recover." But, these benefits of hypertrophy, cardiovascular improvements, and positive immune system response only take place while you rest and recover, *if* you rest and recover. These benefits can't happen *while* we exercise. They can't happen in the gym, and the average recovery for resistance training is 48 to 72 hours per trained muscle group to fully recover and realize the muscular improvements the body was primed for in that specific resistance training workout[1].

For cardiovascular (aerobic) training, there is a less significant recovery period for the heart, but you still need to consider time for joint recovery. Additionally, you need to train for strength at times to maintain muscular balance and optimal joint function – which means even with pure, moderate intensity, cardiovascular focused exercise, rest days will be necessary.

If you insist on exercising for 75 days straight, target a moderate intensity exercise with low physical impact on the joints, such as rowing, cycling, or swimming, while setting aside time for mobility work. However, keep in mind that no balanced fitness program is suitable for 75 continuous days of training.

Exercising for 75 days straight robs us of those recovery processes and health gains, delivering the damage without the development.

Additionally, continually exercising and incrementally breaking down our bodies without time to recover puts us at risk of not only missing the growth we're aiming for but also puts us at increased risk of injury.

Weaker muscles, as happens in overtraining situations, lead to poor form and improperly supported movements. This happens whether lifting weights, running, or playing a sport, and contributes to both usage injuries and injuries from a single activity or trauma during sport or training.

The antidote: Proper rest and active recovery between workouts.

In high-intensity programs, the optimal balance is two days of high-intensity exercise (~20 to 45 minutes) followed by 1 day of active rest that includes stretching and "mobilizing" trouble spots.

For moderate-intensity exercise, such as cardiovascular training like running, swimming, or light rowing, five days of training followed by two days of rest could also be a healthy choice.

We'll get into how to exercise, optimal programs, and how to mobilize later.

For now, we leave at the point that rest is essential to recovery, and 75 days straight of high-intensity exercise puts you at risk of injury and blunts the benefits you will gain. Additionally, athletes doing 2 workouts per day should be at a very advanced level of fitness going in, should have a very specific goal (usually competition) and have a robust coaching, recovery, and nutritional support programs.

MOST "DIETS" AREN'T SUSTAINABLE OR HEALTHY IN THE LONG TERM. HEALTHY EATING HABITS ARE A MORE SUSTAINABLE TARGET WORTH KEEPING

By definition, a diet is "a special course of food to which one restricts oneself, either to lose weight or for medical reasons."

We can see in the definition that the average "diet" serves the very immediate goals of either 1) losing weight or 2) curing a medical condition.

However, what happens when that goal is reached? Most people emerge from their culinary misery feeling deprived and drained, then slowly revert back to old eating habits, which lead to old weights and old medical conditions. Even if they wanted to continue their diet to keep the results, the average popular "diet" with weight loss or health goals in mind isn't sustainable. The diet may be unsustainable for health reasons (risking malnutrition or excessive performance decreases). The diet may be unsustainable due to logistical problems (too much effort to prepare meals and continue with a busy schedule). The diet may also just be impossible to stay motivated during (it's just miserable to maintain)

So, "dieting" towards a healthy weight and life is a problem and nearly impossible challenge on its own for most people.

The solution to the problem of dieting is adopting sustainable and healthy eating habits that we intend to keep and *can* keep in our lives after 75 days. How?

We'll get into our healthier eating guidelines later, but for now realize that fad diets likely aren't the answer to the problem of how to shape and fuel your body long term. Understand that sustainable and healthy eating indefinitely is the answer to shaping the body you want.

THE STRUCTURE OF THE ORIGINAL 75 DAY CHALLENGE FEEDS THE EXPECTATION FOR INSTANTLY OBSERVABLE RESULTS, WHEN IN FACT THE PROCESS IS WHAT MATTERS MOST AND SHOULD BE THE CENTER OF FOCUS.

For long term improvement, attention to the process matters more than attention to results.

The original 75 day challenge tasked participants with taking a picture everyday…to record progress.

On the surface, this may seem like a very benign goal. However, spending 5 to 10 minutes per day taking a half-naked selfie unnecessarily redirects our focus. Instead of focusing on the process and diligently doing what is necessary to create results, we place our focus on progress. This leads to focusing on progress before the process is even near complete and the common, but still unreasonable, expectation that good results happen immediately.

In reality, good, lasting results do not happen immediately. Understanding, internalizing, and applying that valuable lesson to our mindset ultimately leads to a better process.

There is nothing inherently wrong with *tracking* progress. However, daily progress shouldn't be our metric for success. Instead, how often we complete the small actions, diligently continuing the process, should be our metric for success.

You will get more out of your 75 days if you put your head down and simply focus on doing what needs to be done. Just eat healthily, move your body, and practice thankfulness, instead of spending an extra 5 to 10 minutes staring in the mirror or standing on a scale asking, "am I there yet?"

If you use those 5 to 10 minutes to lay in a hammock, relax, or do one of the other tasks, you will stress less if there isn't visible progress yet and you will be one step closer to the result you desire - easily maintained and positive long term habits resulting in a higher quality of life. Even better, you will become more comfortable with doing and trusting the process. You will grow to worry less and trust your diligence more. You will grow trust in, and reliance on, your new habits, relieving your anxiety and freeing a portion of your mind to accomplish more.

Accomplishing a task aimed at bettering you is a significant win. Appreciating that act is much more valuable (in the long term) than examining whether your actions are fruiting benefit, yet.

Our short term goal should be to fall in love with the process and leave the results to their due time (75 days down the road).

THE LIST OF DAILY TASKS IN THE ORIGINAL 75 DAY CHALLENGE MISSES THE OPPORTUNITY FOR "MENTAL HYGIENE" AND MENTAL RECOVERY

The original challenge focused heavily on physical challenge and improvement. We've already mentioned room for intentional, physical recovery. But what about mental recovery?

We can agree that our bodies not only need a day off but also need planned activities to promote recovery (stretching, icing, nutrition, sauna, etc.). But what about our minds? Don't our minds need similar "active recovery" for optimal performance?

To be the best we can be and build the best lives possible, we need to be at our peak, physically and mentally.

To do that, we need to plan mental recovery into our lives to balance challenging ourselves mentally with creating the conditions for mental recovery, and the increased mental strength that comes with it.

The same balance of stretching limits and promoting recovery exists from the standpoint of emotions. If we push ourselves on a daily basis, taxing our minds and pushing the limits of our emotions and patience (as we should), then emotional recovery is just as important, if our goal is peak efficiency and holistic growth.

We can easily build mental hygiene to achieve a clearer, stronger, more focused mind into our 75 days. We can build in emotional hygiene for contentment and to keep that calm, cool, and collected emotional stability that is so valuable in life. We'll build all of this with thankfulness, self-appreciation, mental hygiene to set ourselves up for success in life beyond the 75 days of this program.

The critique above highlights the opportunities for improvement over the original 75-day challenge. Instead of being a simple test that shows we can't be broken, that shows we're tough, we can make it a developmental experience giving us the strength to move through adversity, move obstacles, and move ourselves. We can use the 75 days to "program" universally positive habits we can carry through life.

Ultimately, whether the original 75 day challenge or a more developmental program is more suitable for you depends on your goals, for day 75 and beyond.

If your goal is just to challenge or test grit, the original 75 day challenge may be worth the risks. But there are many other options for achieving the same result without such a significant time investment. We'll share some of those options later.

If the goal is sustainable progression and long-term improvement, we can do better, and we will do better in 75 Strong.

IF YOU ONLY WANT A TEST OF GRIT OR A RUSH TO SNAP YOU OUT OF A RUT, TRY THESE OPTIONS INSTEAD

Seventy-five days is a lot of time to invest to just test or challenge yourself, while receiving little long-term benefit. Instead, I highly recommend these demanding challenges as alternative "rut busters" and personal tests. Each option tests, hones mental strength and builds toughness in a much shorter period than 75 days.

- GORUCK Challenge or local rucking groups
- Run a Spartan Race or other adventure race
- Run a marathon
- Run a triathlon or a sprint triathlon, competitively or on your own
- Do a silent meditation retreat - Sitting still and quiet for 4 to 10 days is a true developmental challenge
- Backpack a continent for 75 days - A taxing, testing, truly educational, and extremely enjoyable experience
- Signup for and run the Barkley Marathon with no hope of finishing.

If you're isolated and can't commit to going somewhere right now, consider these options

- Run your own marathon: 13.1 miles to anywhere and back
- Do a free silent meditation training at home (many are hosted online for free)
- Hike all or a segment of the Pacific Crest Trail or Appalachian Trail
- Go backcountry camping for a week

All of these tasks will push you to the limit in a way that will challenge you, but happen in short enough period that the risk and time investment are low. At the same time, the feeling of accomplishment upon completion will still be high.

I've run an impromptu marathon (alone and in a competition with a few a day's notice), gone on a silent meditation retreat, and gone on a "road to nowhere" motorbike ride for weeks. All of these challenges were sufficiently risky, taxing, and gave me a life jolting adrenaline rush. Some of the experiences didn't lead to lasting positive outcomes - but they didn't consume 75 days either.

There are plenty of short-burst challenges we can do in daily life.

If you're giving something 75 days of your life, ensure it serves your long-term goals

HOW WE'RE RESTRUCTURING OUR 75 DAY PROGRAM: WE'LL PLAN TO BUILD FOUNDATIONAL HABITS, GRIT, AND STRENGTH PHYSICALLY AND MENTALLY

For all of their flaws, the popular and original 75 day challenges had *a lot* of potential. Anything that shocks us out of bad habits and adds good habits is a great start. But to make the 75 day commitment healthy and worthwhile, we still needed to change a few things before jumping in.

So, what will we adapt and improve to create a more beneficial 75 day challenge?

TWO WORKOUTS A DAY IS RISKY – WE'LL GO WITH ONE WORKOUT PER DAY.

Beyond one workout per day, there is little benefit and higher risk of injury. Athletes training for a Crossfit competition, professional spors, or the Olympics may do this. However, these elite athletes likely have a coach, support team, nutritional resources, and a recovery plan that you don't and a very advanced level of fitness going into their "two a day, every day" training regimen. Sticking to one "all-in" workout on workout days is the optimal approach for maximum benefit and minimal risk.

SEVENTY-FIVE DAYS OF INTENSE EXERCISE WITHOUT REST IS RISKY. SCHEDULE RECOVERY DAYS: TWO DAYS OF EXERCISE, ONE DAY OF REST.

Worthwhile and intense exercise breaks your body down slightly. More importantly, intense exercise stimulates recovery mechanisms and useful immune system response. Efficient exercise stimulates our bodies and signals, to our body's recovery systems, that the strength, mobility, and cardiovascular health we currently have needs to be maintained or improved. In the rest periods between workouts, a cascade of hormonal, metabolic, and immune responses take place to rebuild our bodies, maintaining that strength and cardiovascular fitness and burning pesky fat along the way.

The important thing to remember is that these recovery processes, and the accompanying growth and improvement, only happen *when* you *rest*. If you exercise for 75 days straight, you are robbing yourself of this valuable recovery period in which growth and improvement take place, ultimately blunting your fitness gains. At worst, you are weakening yourself and moving closer to potential injury day by day. Plus, if you go too hard and injure yourself on day 40, you won't make it through the process long enough to see the *true* benefits of day 75 and the newly ingrained long term habit of daily exercise and healthy movement.

EATING GUIDELINES DURING THE 75 DAY CHALLENGE

The term "diet" is too vague and a potential trap for counterproductive diet trends. Instead, we'll choose specific, universally healthy eating habits suited to you, to carry past 75 days.

In the original 75 day challenge, there was a general suggestion to "follow a diet." The problem with this well-intentioned advice is most "diets" are fads passed around on the internet based on little science and lots of conjecture. These diets may result in a pound or two lost now but are ultimately unsustainable long term due to health or interest reasons. Instead, from an eating and nutrition standpoint, it's much more valuable to be clear about what types of foods are generally detrimental to our health and eliminate them from our eating plan, and identify foods that offer needed fuel and nutrients with minimal negative side effects and *add* those foods to our eating guidelines.

The past challenges weren't specific enough about what to eat, when to eat, or how much to eat, to achieve the goals of our program – healthy bodyweight, a smooth running body, and the high energy levels that come from eating healthily – so we'll clarify what to eat, how much to eat, and when to eat in our eating guidelines.

Not being specific about an approach to nutrition is at best a wasted opportunity and, at worst, a trap potentially detrimental to our health. Not choosing specific science-backed healthy eating guidelines is equally wasteful. Also, our eating plan should take into account our fitness approach and long-term goals.

To correct this, we'll select universally healthy eating guidelines that have been proven to lead to a healthier body. We'll ensure each potential guideline is sustainable and aim to incorporate the eating guidelines as a habit in the long term.

A PREVIOUS 75 DAY CHALLENGE RECOMMENDED TAKING A PROGRESS PICTURE OF YOURSELF EVERYDAY.

Taking a picture of yourself every day is a potentially negative distractor from the process, perpetuating the instant gratification focused mentality. Instead, we'll put our attention fully on the process.

Focusing on the process and completing the task in front of us diligently is far more beneficial to our aims than checking for progress each day. The pursuit of long-term change should embrace a proven, reliable process (daily habits in this case) and ignore the results until the end.

Instead of taking a daily picture, take a picture once at the beginning of the 75 days and once at the end. Along the way, we'll use our checklist to ensure we're completing the "daily 10" tasks and optional journal to record valuable thoughts. If you put a check in the box for your task, that's all the progress we need to worry about. Accept that and be proud of yourself.

Use that daily checklist, with your checks in the boxes as your proof that you're doing the work, not a selfie, and let that be enough. Understand that the results will come. If you have done the work each day, you have results to be proud of. You don't need a picture to distract you from that.

Now that we've identified and navigated around potential trouble spots in our 75 day program let's add some daily tasks to build on it and make the most of our 75 day investment.

WHAT WE'LL ADD FOR OUR 75 DAY PROGRAM

- One workout per day maximum
- Program rest and recovery days and emphasis on not just exercise but recovery, stretching, and improving mobility
- Choose specific, healthy eating guidelines that we can keep long term without losing our sanity
- Personalize the rules and goals of the challenge to include your personal desires and goals
- Practice habits and routines that we'll want to keep after day 75
- Keep a checklist, checking off tasks each day as proof of our progress

WHAT THE ORIGINAL 75 DAY CHALLENGE DOES WELL THAT WE'LL KEEP GOING

Despite the important points for improvement listed above, the original 75 day challenge had a lot of good already built-in. Working out routinely, skipping alcohol, and building a habit of absorbing knowledge daily are all great.

We will continue these good points and build on them.

The most significant tasks that we want to keep from the original 75 day challenges are:

- Building that "long term commitment" and grit muscle

- Breaking us out of a rut and ditching poor habits
- Building healthy, sustainable habits
- Pursuing health through what we eat
- Pursuing fitness, for functional and health reasons
- Skipping alcohol
- Pursuing knowledge and exposure to varied ideas

CHAPTER 2: A 75 DAY PROGRAM TO LIFELONG STRENGTH

For the next 75 days, you will complete each of the "Daily 10" tasks 9 out of every 10 days. Here are the 10 tasks you'll complete:

THE DAILY 10

1. **Be Thankful:** List 20 things you're thankful for, written or aloud

2. **Self-Appreciation:** List 20 things you appreciate about yourself, written or aloud

3. **Be Still:** Sit in silence and stillness for 15 minutes

4. **Move:** Exercise daily for 2 days, then take 1 day to recover and stretch, then repeat

5. **Eat Healthily**
   - Eat meat and vegetables, nuts and seeds, some fruit, no processed sugar, minimal refined carbs, low starch
   - Consider intermittent fasting by eating within an 8 to 12 hour window daily (Consult your physician before

taking on this task)

6. Skip Alcohol: Aim to drink no alcohol for 75 days straight

7. Read: Read or listen to a book for 15 minutes

8. Learn: Study or practice a new skill or concept for at least 15 minutes

9. Express a Passion: Do something that you are passionate about and that enlivens you, and is not related to your work, for at least 15 minutes

10. Embrace (and Record) the Process: Check off all tasks completed in your checklist and record your thoughts, feelings, and realizations daily in a journal.

Every day you will aim to complete 9 of these 10 tasks at *minimum*.

The tasks of not drinking alcohol, moving every day (working out or stretching), and recording (and embracing) the process are non-negotiable and must be done every day. This is because these tasks will have the most benefit in your life, and they will likely be the tasks you'll want to break the most – and we're not having that. Additionally, these will be the hardest tasks for most people to adapt to and make habit. As such, stay the course to ingrain these tasks as habits (or reprogrammed habits) sooner.

Why are we allowing you to *miss* tasks 1 day of every 10 if this program is about diligence?

The primary goal of this program is not to "beat a challenge." The goal of this program is to build a foundation of positive *habits* that will make you physically, mentally, and emotionally stronger and improve your quality of life. To calculate for that, we use two findings from a study performed by Phillipa Lally at the University

College of London (Lally)[2]. The findings revealed:

1. On average, it takes 66 days to build a true habit, not the 21 days commonly quoted. If you accomplish your tasks 9 days of every 10 in the challenge (90% of the time), you pass the average threshold for making a repeated action a habit, with 67 days and repetitions per task.

2. Missing a *single* day of a task over an extended period doesn't negatively affect how ingrained the habit becomes. Accounting for a missed task repetition 1 of every 10 days allows sufficient flex for human imperfection and unexpected events in everyday life.

We're not perfect. Lives are dynamic. We can build strength and adaptability while accounting for that.

We'll go into each element of our Daily 10 in-depth, but first, let's examine the model we're using to inspire our 75 days to a stronger you program.

CHAPTER 3: 8 TENETS FOR THE CHALLENGE AND LIFE

75 Strong is all about building a foundation of habits and routines to help you build a higher quality of life from the ground up. But even foundations have something holding them up.

The Daily 10 tasks are great habits, specific actions to maintain in your daily life. Beneath those, these eight tenets underpin what we are trying to achieve and how we're trying to achieve it. To go further, these principles are fantastic for shaping your life. The 8 tenets that follow shape the spirit of our challenge and will be the guiding spirit of our efforts over the next 75 days.

Think of the Daily 10 tasks as the "tactics" and specific actions we do every day to drive us to our goal – a stronger you, mentally and physically.

Think of the following tenets as the "strategy," overarching ideas we use to guide the campaign of our lives. If you come to a fork in the road with your tasks during the 75 day challenge and you're not sure which way to go, come back to these tenets to break the tie and guide you onto the best path.

Here are our guiding tenets in the 75 Strong program:

1. All things in moderation.
2. Focus on small, consistent actions to achieve big accomplishments. Remember, grains of sand form beaches.
3. Fall in love with diligently completing the process, not the result, and then the desired result will come naturally.
4. Your time, energy, and passion are valuable resources that no one can take away from you and you can only give them freely. Invest your time, energy, and passion accordingly, with the long term in mind and guard them unapologetically.
5. Program positive habits until they have become automatic, taking minimal effort. This is how we accrue wins, in the long term, through the aggregate of positive, near effortless action.
6. 90% is solid. Perfection is impossible and unnecessary. Act accordingly. Perform, acknowledge, move on.
7. Decide what you won't compromise on and act accordingly.

Now, let's dig a little deeper into the 8 tenets of our 75 day challenge

ALL THINGS IN MODERATION

Very few things in life are 100% bad. At the same moment, very few things in life are 100% good.

Exercise, in moderation with a good recovery protocol, creates a durable, capable, injury-resistant body. Exercise in excess breaks us beyond repair.

A glass of wine in moderation is a delightful social lubricant and quick shortcut to relaxing with moderate health benefits. Wine in excess damages our bodies and paralyzes our minds.

Ambition and drive in moderation push us to action that leads to the goals and rewards that leave us feeling fulfilled on an individual basis. Ambition and drive in excess leave us unfulfilled, covetous, and almost neurotic in our obsession with forward progress, unable to enjoy the gift of being still for a moment.

The point?

Most things can be good if experienced in (relative) moderation. And all things can be harmful in excess. Judge what you commit to and restrain from accordingly.

According to the philosopher Aristotle:

"The virtuous habit of action is always an intermediate state between the opposed vices of excess and deficiency."

In daily life, if you desire a healthy life, strive for balance in all things. The middle ground of moderation is where you will find the best and strongest version of yourself.

FOCUS ON SMALL, CONSISTENT ACTIONS TO ACHIEVE BIG RESULTS. REMEMBER GRAINS OF SAND FORM BEACHES.

In the age of the internet, quick wins, and get-rich-quick opportunities, most people obsess over opportunities for "big wins" achieved via "massive action." Most people lust over those huge payoffs that they hope deliver a windfall of riches and an accompanying adrenaline rush.

As sexy as overnight success seems, it is rare. Additionally, few things that come quickly actually last.

Some of the greatest things in life that last are built diligently over time. Healthy bodies. Healthy relationships. Empires that outlive their founders. Small actions, almost imperceptible to bystanders in the moment, form the foundations of real lasting success.

The beautiful beaches that many of us lust after aren't made of huge boulders, they're made of many tiny grains of sand crushed and passively gathered over millions of years.

The road to lasting success carries the same structure. Lasting success is made of tiny actions executed diligently, sustainably, over an extended period of time, ultimately forming larger, more visible "achievements" when viewed in aggregate.

Some of those tiny actions contribute significantly. Some actions contribute very little directly to the end state. Some actions are never seen by others. However, every single tiny action is a step in *your* process.

Your favorite mogul likely slaved on their project for minutes, hours, and days, performing mundane tasks before anyone recognized their name.

For master-level achievers that have put in their 10,000 hours, every single minute of those 10,000 hours was a diligent grain of sand in their beach of success, each minute, built on the previous minute, a brick in their castle of success.

Massive action sounds sexy; I realize that.

But small, unfalteringly consistent actions are what create reliable results.

Small actions are possible when you're tired, when you lack confidence, and when you're confused about the road far ahead. Small actions are *always* possible. Thus, when built with small actions, success is always possible.

It's ok to think and dream big.

And it's ok to focus on small actions to get there.

Small actions in your 75 days

As you perform your "Daily 10" actions over the next 75 days, for minutes at a time, you will get bored. This will feel mundane at some point. You will want to skip a task or a day. You may even want to quit.

Don't.

Each task completed and each box checked is a small action, a proverbial stone, contributing to the foundation of the stronger you.

Small actions in life

Spoiler alert: You will fail. You will be tired. You will very rarely be functioning at 100%

This is not an excuse to stop.

When you hit low points in life and when you feel you have nothing left, look for some small action to do. Do it without obsessing over the result – just doing it is a win. Then, move on to the next small action.

The mountain in front of you may look impossible to climb, but you don't have to climb the mountain. That isn't your goal now. For now, you just need to take one step. You can figure out what follows, where to go next, and how to do it, later. For now, just take one step.

Move and keep moving...with small actions.

FALL IN LOVE WITH THE PROCESS

You'll win some, you'll lose some, but on average, you'll win. If you focus on the result, the losses will hurt harder than they should. If you focus on the process, the losses won't matter because by continuing the process, you're winning. Always winning.

Falling in love with the process in this program

The process in this challenge is simply doing your actions daily. This is despite whether you're shedding pounds, despite whether you *feel* smarter, and despite whether your 1-mile time has dropped.

Your goal is to execute diligently every day. That's it. If you are executing, you are programming positive habits that will stick with you for years. If you execute on that process, you're winning.

Focus on the process, not the result.

Falling in love with the process in life

As long as you have identified a path, and a process on that path that suits your ethos and your goals, stay focused and just *do*.

If you appreciate your job, show up on time and execute as best as you can every day. Do as much as you can, and be happy with that. Regardless of what anyone says or doesn't say.

If you love and are committed to your partner or your children, then love them as you know you want to. Regardless of their moodiness, their hurdles, or their chaos, that isn't your fault, fall in love with the process of loving them.

If you are committed to staying fit, fall in love with the idea of putting on those shoes, going for a run, and feeling your heart pump and lungs swell. Perform the action diligently for *that* reason...not for the anticipated result. Do that, and results will come without the anxiety.

The warning with this is ensure you are committed to a process that is true to you, your ethos, and your goals. Committing your whole self to someone else's process (instead of your own) is a road to ruin.

However, if the process (and path) is yours, commit to it, do it, and love it.

YOUR TIME, ENERGY, AND PASSION ARE VALUABLE RESOURCES THAT NO ONE CAN TAKE AWAY. INVEST THEM ACCORDINGLY WITH THE LONG TERM IN MIND.

As far as I know, you get one life. I may be wrong, but let's roll with that assumption for the sake of this point.

In this life, many things can be forcibly taken from you; your home, your money, even your job. However, time, energy, and passion cannot be taken from you by anyone, without your permission. You have to give them willingly if anyone else is to benefit from them.

In the same moment, time, energy, and passion are the three most valuable resources you have in this life.

Any other asset – money, material resources, organizations, technology, etc. – is built with time, energy, and passion.

Every billionaire, professional athlete, or successful person you can think of built their empire with their time, energy, and passion in some varied mixture with a significant portion of each.

You have the same amount of time on this planet as most people.

You have the same amount of energy as most people (and you can cultivate more if you wish).

You have as much passion as most people (and you can cultivate more if you wish).

You have the ingredients to build the empires you admire. Don't waste them - time, energy, or passion - on any cause or goal that isn't true to your path.

TIME, ENERGY, AND PASSION IN THIS PROGRAM

Seventy-five days is a significant amount of time. If you are going to commit to 75 days of work, ensure the goal (a foundation of positive habits) is what you want after 75 days.

If a foundation of positive habits isn't your goal, congratulations on that realization. DO NOT do this program. Instead, find something that suits your goals to do for 75 days.

If a foundation of positive habits is your goal, then intentionally invest your time, energy, and passion over the next 75 days.

Judiciously investing your time, energy, and passions in life

Time management will be a significant issue over the next 75 days. To accomplish your goal of 75 days of consistency, you will have to say no – to people, to desires, to activities. Do it unapologetically, wasting no energy apologizing as you do what's best for you and what leads to a better you.

Life, and every moment in it, is too valuable to spend doing ANYTHING that doesn't suit your purpose, your goals, your desires, and your ethos.

Learn to say a hard "no" unapologetically as often as you need to. Then reinvest that time, energy, and passion into something you want to see flourish.

PROGRAM POSITIVE HABITS UNTIL THEY BECOME AUTONOMIC. THIS IS HOW WE ACCRUE LOW EFFORT WINS IN THE LONG TERM.

"Tasks" not only take the effort required to perform the task but also the effort of motivating yourself to act. This is in addition to the mental energy required to plan when to do the task and how exactly you'll do that task.

Though you may not realize it, the process of starting a task takes a lot of extra effort compared to the relatively low effort required to act on a habit.

On the other hand, a habit *does* require the energy of performing that task, but that's it. You don't need to take the energy to motivate yourself to do a habit or the mental energy necessary to plan how to execute the habit, because the habit has become a part of you. There is a pull. You *need* to do it.

A habit is instinctive and automatic. Your body and unconscious mind know how to perform the habit without you remembering the "how."

Habits don't need to be planned into your day. Habits, especially if they're programmed as routines, are so ingrained that your body and mind can launch into them at the right time without any complex thought.

For these reasons, every potential positive task we would like to do, we also want to make a habit – an autonomic action we can perform with minimal effort.

We want to make being thankful for everything, and existing in a state of contentment, a habit.

We want to make self-appreciation, and the accompanying act of being confident in ourselves and capabilities, a habit.

We want to make moving our bodies and the fitness that comes with it a habit.

By making all of these essential tasks habits, we're taking steps to ensure we'll still be benefitting from our 75 days of effort years down the road.

Performing each of these positive actions as habits frees up mental energy, emotional energy, and motivation to take on other one-off "tasks" that lead to other goals, while keeping the positive momentum we'll have at the end of the 75 days.

Programming positive habits in this program and in life

By doing this challenge and completing the tasks at a 90% level over the 75 days, you are building a foundation of 10 extremely beneficial habits. 66 days of action, that's all we need.

Just stick to, and fall in love with the process.

90% IS SOLID. PERFECTION IS IMPOSSIBLE AND UNNECESSARY. ACT ACCORDINGLY. PERFORM, ACKNOWLEDGE, MOVE ON.

You will fail. That is ok. Even good.

Failures are the lectures of life. If you pay attention, you'll learn a valuable lesson.

In this challenge, "perfection" would involve performing every single task every day for 75 days. If you hit that, good. That's amazing.

If you only make 9 out of 10 tasks before you go to sleep, but you made 9, all is good. However, sit down and ask yourself why you missed the last task? What could you have done differently? What non-essential activity or time-waster during the day could you eliminate to make room for that beneficial task you skipped? Then learn from the moment and let it go.

We're not striving for perfection. We're just striving for better.

All things in moderation, right?

Don't pressure yourself to do *everything* perfectly.

However, do hold yourself accountable to doing the things well that you commit to.

Hit that 90% mark.

Aiming for 90% in this program

Perfection isn't our goal. Concerted effort and continual improvement are our goals. Maintaining the balanced approach of slight tolerance for error (and the unexpected) by missing a task once every ten days while pushing ourselves to be accountable to a higher-than-normal standard will bring out the best version of ourselves.

We've also discussed how, on average, 66 days create a habit. By maintaining our standard of 90%, by day 75 we will have completed 67 repetitions and breached the average threshold for making a task a habit, and we will have ingrained 10 new, highly beneficial habits into our life.

Aiming for 90% in life

No matter what you're doing in life, the first 80% will be the easiest part, requiring the least amount of relative effort. Completing the remaining 20% will take everything else out of you.

We don't necessarily need that remaining 20% as it's often not worth the opportunity cost to pursue the remaining 20%.

However, striving beyond the "easy part," the first 80% for an extra 10%, conditions us to do more than average, to go above and beyond in whatever we do for higher quality, and produces better results as a byproduct.

In whatever you do, don't fall into the neurosis of obsessing over the possibility of perfection.

However, do condition yourself to instinctively give that extra 10% once things get hard. If you continue giving that until it becomes a habit it won't be hard anymore.

67 days.

90%.

That's what we're after.

DECIDE WHAT YOU WON'T COMPROMISE ON, THEN DON'T

Every person should have an ethos, standards, values, and priorities that they won't compromise on. In hard times, having a well-defined ethos will make it easy to stand firm on the things you won't compromise on and keep pushing through the storm even when you're at your weakest. This way, when your strength has returned, or the storm subsides, you will still be proud of your actions, and even at your weakest points, your actions will contribute to the better you and *your* process.

Just remember, we create our shelters before the storm, and we define our ethos before the hard times.

Decide now what you won't compromise on. Then, don't, unapologetically. You don't need to reason, rationalize, or explain to anyone. Build your ethos, internalize it, and live by it. Do. Not. Compromise.

Deciding on what you won't compromise on in this program

Look at the list of tasks now and decide definitively which ones you are committing to, then stand firm.

You'll have friends that say, "just come for a beer."

You'll have friends that kindly offer a slice of pizza even though it is outside of your eating guidelines.

You'll have social engagements that interfere with getting in your workout.

Say no.

These actions, the daily 10 habits we are aiming to build, are part of the process that leads to your goal. Do not compromise on them; politely refuse anything that stands in the way. If the pressure keeps coming, unapologetically say no, stand firm, and be proud in that you're putting in a little extra effort to stick to your process.

CHAPTER 4: TIPS FOR A SUCCESSFUL CHALLENGE

The next 75 days of action *will* be a challenge - in completing the actions themselves, in time management, and in staying disciplined.

In this chapter, we'll review some tips to help you stick to and make it through this 75 day challenge.

The Tips:

- **Stack your morning with the tasks that give you energy** and positive momentum to carry you through the day
- **Plan a time management approach** that works best for you. Time management will be vital to squeezing in all of the tasks each day.
- **Pull someone else in.** This thing gets 10 times easier with support and a team. If you have 5 people doing the 75 day challenge with you, you'll have significantly more motivation and support compared to going solo. Even

if friends and family aren't doing the challenge with you, letting them know your intentions gives them the opportunity to support you and keep you accountable when your willpower is running low.

- **Make the goal of the challenge internalizing positive habits.** Don't make the challenge goal to lose weight. If you internalize healthy habits from the challenge, the beneficial changes (such as weight loss) will happen on their own over time. For now, focus on the process.

- **Use this challenge as a positive catalyst** and an excuse to break out of bad habits and into intentional, positive new routines. End your night at a healthy time, wake up early, skip the piece of cake, and capitalize on any other opportunities for improvement that pop up.

- **Don't be afraid to say "no" to others so you can stay on track for you.** Internalize that habit. "Sorry, can't drink, I'm doing a challenge." Or say "I have to head out now, going to bed early so I can workout tomorrow morning." Use your commitment to the challenge as an excuse to do whatever is necessary maintain your progress.

- **Make this challenge your own.** Adapt the tasks and structure as you need in order to live how you want and achieve what you need to achieve. If you need to have that small piece of carrot cake each night to make the other nine tasks doable, do it. Just be sure to do some extra kettlebell swings. If you only pick one of these tasks for 75 days, do it. If this challenge is too light and you need to add 10 more tasks to your Daily 10, do it. Make this challenge yours. Do what's best for you.

- **For everything you're removing from your life in this challenge, replace the loss with something beneficial.** Removing alcohol? Intentionally replace the drink with club soda or smoothies. Skipping social time at the bar? Be sure to meet up with a friend for dinner or a hike. Any void in your time and your life will naturally get filled. If you don't fill it deliberately, you're relying on chance and luck to fill it with something aligned with your goals. Don't take that chance, be intentional with what fills your life.

- **Think small**. In this day and age, we're encouraged to "think big." Too often we assume if something isn't 10x more significant than the previous version, it isn't noteworthy, and isn't worth celebrating. Get that out of your head. When it comes to the actions in this challenge, start small, then grow. Learn to crawl, then walk, then run, and celebrate each step of that process.

MY PERSONAL EXPERIENCE WITH THE 75 STRONG CHALLENGE

Like many people over the past years, I adapted to the new normal. I accepted that there were fewer opportunities and external motivations to live my "old normal" life. Fewer healthy habits took the place of my lost routines and many detrimental habits stacked on top of my existing bad habits.

As I shared before, after a stint of isolation, I popped out of my cave with my surfboard. Eyes squinting in the unfamiliar sunlight, and charged into the waves. My first realization was, "Wow! How did I get this out of shape!"

That was my "lightbulb moment," when reality became a lot clearer.

I realized I was writing less, running less, and reading less. The banality of my limited routines stifled my motivation and led to a state with little forward movement, which is essentially moving backwards. Nothing was quite *broken,* but I had the potential to be better. I had the potential to *do* better.

That's when I reassessed, recalibrated, and rebuilt my routines and standards.

Whether I realized it or not, that was the first day of my 75 Strong challenge

MY RESULTS: A RETURN TO FORWARD MOTION

For me, the tasks in the 75 Strong challenge have gone from being grueling and unnatural to becoming a daily practice that delivers constant, gradual improvement. My satisfaction with the challenge, and the results I've seen and felt from the challenge have continued to increase long after my first 75 days.

After months of routine workouts (I chose the 10,000 Kettlebell Swing Challenge followed by a gymnastics and calisthenics protocol), no alcohol, and skipping refined carbs, I lost 6 pounds and felt stronger than ever. My sleep patterns and mental focus improved immensely. I regained a love of reading - choosing books over streaming tv shows - and my mood is better than I can remember.

The challenge's benefits are well worth the sacrifice of effort and time and the habits continue to stick effortlessly well after the challenge's end.

WHY I DESIGNED THE 75 STRONG CHALLENGE

Building healthy, productive long-term habits is one of the hardest things to do, but one of the best things we can do. That's what this challenge about. That's what I want others to make their 75 days about as well.

Challenges are normally about the rush of toughing it out,

completion, and bragging rights. But eventually, we "rebound" and return to our old habits, losing our gains.

This book was written to suggest a 75-day exercise in reprogramming base, effective, healthy habits physically, mentally, and emotionally.

If you take on this 75 day challenge and want to share your experiences with me, feel free to find and contact me at ABrotherAbroad.com

I'll look forward to hearing about your results on the other side.

Good luck.

"DAILY 10" RECAP

Here's a reminder of the "Daily 10" tasks we'll do every day for 75 days straight

1. Be Thankful: List 20 things you're thankful for, written or aloud

2. **Self-Appreciation:** List 20 things you appreciate about yourself, written or aloud

3. **Be Still:** Sit in silence and stillness for 15 minutes

4. **Move and mobilize** by working out for 2 days, then taking 1 day to recover and stretch, then repeating

5. **Eat Healthily**

- Eat meat and vegetables, nuts and seeds, some fruit, no processed sugar, minimal refined carbs, low starch
- Consider intermittent fasting by eating within an 8 to 12 hour window daily (talk to your physician before taking on this task)

6. **Skip alcohol** completely for the 75 days

7. **Read or listen to a book** for 15 minutes

8. **Learn a new concept or skill** for 15 minutes

9. **Express a passion** for 15 minutes

10. **Record the process** daily in a journal and note your wins of completing tasks in a checklist

Now, we will go in-depth into each 1 of our 10 daily tasks. We'll detail not only why each is part of our challenge but also why each is a potential habit we should build into our lives as effortless action.

CHAPTER 5: THE 75 STRONG DAILY TASKS, IN-DEPTH

Let's dig into each of our "Daily 10" tasks for the next 75 days.

Every task is sustainable indefinitely.

Every task improves our bodies, our minds, our emotions, and our lives just by performing it.

Every task is a potential habit, and a positive one, if ingrained deeply enough and performed consistently.

Every time you succeed in doing a task and being diligent in the process, you're improving.

Our goal isn't *just* to get to 75 days. Our goal is to make each task in our "Daily 10" so reflexive that after the 75 days, we will continue doing them effortlessly.

66 DAYS CREATE A HABIT

It is commonly stated that 21 days of repeating a task creates a habit. This is a constantly repeated misunderstanding.

In 1960, Dr. Maxwell Maltz observed that surgery patients that had limbs removed and body parts altered took 21 days to get *familiar* with seeing and feeling the new versions of themselves. This did not mean it felt natural or second nature after 21 days; the body part simply did not feel as strange and foreign as at the beginning.

So, it takes 21 days to build familiarity, not to build a habit.

Familiarity means doing the action doesn't feel abnormal. That is not what we're after.

It takes 66 days of repeating a task, on average, to make a habit.

Special operations soldiers, skilled surgeons, and professional athletes aren't "familiar" with their actions and common tasks of their trade; they are "ingrained" with the habits that make them successful. For them, the tasks of their trade are reflexive habits.

We desire to create habits. Our goal is for every single one of the Daily 10 tasks to feel so essential that doing the prescribed action feels effortless, and not doing the action feels abnormal.

In reality, research has shown that it takes 66 days, on average, to create a habit.

A study performed by researcher Phillippa Lally at the University College London determined that an action becomes a habit after completing it over 66 separate days on average. The study also found that occasionally missing a day didn't hinder the creation of the habit. (Lally)[3]

This research details why our challenge is 75 days long.

WHY IS THIS CHALLENGE 75 DAYS?

75 Days x 90% Performance = 67 Days of Action Per Task = Just beyond the repetition threshold for making an action a habit

Completing every task 9 out of 10 times we have the opportunity to perform each task 67 times in 75 days, a period tight enough to make our target action a habit.

This puts us just above the average threshold for *truly* making the actions habit.

75 days of diligent action, with room for human error, to create a better life and a stronger you.

Now, let's dig into the "Daily 10" actions that will change your life and why we're doing them.

DAILY TASK #1: BE THANKFUL

How: Start each day listing 20 things you're thankful for, written or aloud

You can remember and express your 20 things to be thankful for in the shower, while you're making breakfast, or even before you get out of bed.

THE SCIENCE AND BENEFITS OF BEING THANKFUL

- Studies show that grateful people experience more positive emotions, fewer negative emotions, less depression, less anxiety, and get less caught up pursuing materialist goals that don't suit their long term objectives. (McCullough)[4]

Research[5] into the effects of practicing gratefulness via writing and its effects on mental health revealed the following findings:

- Participants that practiced daily gratitude via a gratitude writing exercise were reported to have significantly better mental health than study participants who did not practice gratitude
- Even 12 weeks after the study and ceasing the gratitude exercise, gratitude practicing participants were still reported to have significantly better mental health than counterpart groups
- Practicing gratitude improves brain function in the regions such as the hypothalamus, which secretes dopamine, oxytocin, and endorphin

WHY PRACTICE THANKFULNESS IN THE MORNING

The intentional positive actions of practicing gratefulness and the state of being grateful trigger a release of dopamine, serotonin, and positive hormones at the start of the day, creating positive momentum physically, emotionally, and mentally, that will help us excel even more at the easy and natural tasks throughout our day. Additionally, the positive start will help us weather trying and testing problems throughout the day with more resilience.

Beyond the hormonal benefits, practicing thankfulness places our focus on the positive aspects of our life that we want to grow – and that awareness of what we have that we want to protect and grow is the first step to take in preserving and increasing the aspects of our life that we're thankful for. Setting the target of our focus early in the day gives us more time each day to act on that focus, the realizations, and the opportunities that come with it.

Last, from a practical standpoint, if our limited field of vision is focused on the positive and being positive it leaves less mental capacity to focus on the negative, effectively eliminating the negative from our field of you view in an anxiety reducing and worry reducing way. By starting early, we push the unnecessary negative points out of our vision early on.

If you are alive and breathing right now, you have a lot to be thankful for. You likely have clean water to drink. You'll likely have a meal within a few hours of reading this. You likely have at least a few relationships that are filled with support, mutual love, and pleasure, you likely have a job, opportunities to travel, opportunities to do what you love, money in your pocket, hobbies, passions, etc. and so much more.

At the very least, you have the ability to enact any change in your life that you truly want in the long term.

Why are we practicing thankfulness?

You have much to be thankful for in your life already. However, appreciating that fact and reaping the benefits that come from that appreciation require intention. Being grateful is a habit that you can practice and gratefulness is a state you can consciously place yourself in (through the action of expressing gratefulness). Even better, just as the research showed gratefulness practitioners experiencing the benefits of being thankful even months after the exercise ceased, we can condition ourselves to exist in the state with minimal effort and reap the benefits past 75 days.

As the research shows, that state of gratefulness changes our brain, how it exists and how it functions, and correlates with more positive emotions. These positive states, with less worrying, less anxiety, and less depression, make us more effective, more resilient, and more productive in alignment with our individual goals – ultimately making us mentally and emotionally stronger.

Suppose you are intentionally and consciously aware of all of the fantastic things that already exist in your life. If you are of the things you *could* be appreciative of then you're more likely to appreciate them, more likely to feel more content in general, and more likely to maintain a positive and empowering outlook as a result of this conscious gratefulness. Your outlook will then likely be based in this thankfulness and appreciation for what you already have around you, instead of covetousness, want, and discontent. That state correlates with lower anxiety, worry and depression, automatically setting you up for higher performance.

Saying aloud, or writing, 20 things you're grateful for every morning jumpstarts your day in a positive, empowering way and puts you in a headspace of appreciation and strength regardless of what comes your way.

The things we focus on fill our vision and our minds and affect our contentment or discontentment accordingly. Focus on what you don't have, what you hate, and what you wish was different, and you will experience a flood of negative emotions and hormones just as if what you were envisioning was happening in that moment. Because of this, your propensity for anxiety, sadness, worry, and other counterproductive emotional states will soar. Concentrating on things we are already lucky to have and want more of in our lives puts attention on those things in a way that helps them grow.

If you have a relationship you're appreciative of and express that then I guarantee that relationship will flourish. If you have a hobby that makes you feel enlivened and you're conscious of its value in your life, I guarantee you'll make more time to practice it and experience the positive benefits of immersing yourself in something you are passionate about. If you're grateful for your body, you're more likely to exercise and maintain it. All of these actions, rooted in gratefulness, create a positive feedback loop. Positive thoughts create positive states and emotions which feed productive actions that feed positive thoughts, continuing the cycle. When you accomplish tasks in the way you desire, your brain releases more dopamine which has positive results and feeds positive emotions which fuel positive actions.

Intentional thankfulness in our lives is a form of emotional hygiene. Expressing thankfulness keeps us grounded in reality and focused on the important things. This ensures we give adequate attention to opportunities for happiness and contentment during rough times, instead of becoming distracted with discomfort or focused on the things we don't have.

In the good, peaceful times, this conscious, intentional thankfulness can be a reminder to reinvest in and grow the things we are grateful for and taking nothing for granted. In the hard times, gratefulness will keep us fueled as we continue to fight the good fight and focus on the light at the end of the tunnel.

Perhaps you're thankful for a brother or sister that you haven't called in weeks. That acknowledgment of gratefulness could spark the initiative to call, adding positivity to your day, as well as theirs.

Perhaps you're thankful for a hobby – such as gardening, or painting, or volunteering – but it has been deprioritized because you haven't been *intentional* with your time. This acknowledgment could be the spark for you to start into that passion again offering a much-needed mental escape to your day.

The figurative plants that we water and give attention to grow the most to fill the metaphorical gardens of our lives, whether they're weeds or fruiting trees. Being consciously and intentionally thankful for the fruiting elements in our lives will not only lead to a more realistically positive outlook but will guide you to invest energy and focus and invest more in the things you want more of.

SHOULD YOU FIND 20 *NEW* THINGS TO EXPRESS THANKFULNESS FOR EACH DAY?

Ideally, yes. Each day, highlight 20 *new* things that you're thankful for. If you can't think of 20 new things then this exercise will be that much more effective. You absolutely have 20 things to be thankful for however they are so buried from your awareness that you may *feel* like they're not even there.

Push yourself to become aware of those new 20 things that you have completely forgotten or weren't aware of. By doing that, you are effectively adding 20 brand new things that you appreciate to your life.

Do that for 75 days straight, and you'll have a lot to be thankful for.

TAKEAWAYS ON BEING THANKFUL

- Practice thankfulness each morning by listing 20 specific things you are thankful for finding 20 new things each day
- People who practice thankfulness have been observed in clinical studies to more frequently feel positive emotions and are less likely to feel negative states like anxiousness or worry
- Thankful people are less likely to waste time pursuing materialistic goals that don't fit their own long-term vision
- Practicing thankfulness contributes to the positive mental and emotional foundation that makes you more mentally and emotionally resilient and, ultimately, stronger

DAILY TASK #2: APPRECIATE YOURSELF

How: List 20 things you appreciate about yourself

Every day, highlight 20 things that you appreciate about yourself - on paper or aloud - to give yourself the credit you deserve and to remind yourself to keep repeating what is working. The ego boost will be nice, but you'll remind yourself to "keep on keeping on" by continuing to *do more* of what makes you awesome. That's how you're going to improve the "gardens" that are your mind, your body, and your life in a sustainable, efficient, fulfilling way.

Remind yourself of all the things about yourself that are worth appreciating. State 20 reasons why you're awesome and why you appreciate yourself. These 20 things could include traits, past actions or achievements, or anything else positive. Start it in the morning, end the day with it, or just sprinkle the compliments throughout your day.

THE SCIENCE AND BENEFITS OF APPRECIATING YOURSELF

- A study showed self-appreciation and positive self-

talk are effective for driving positive cognitive and behavioral changes as well as internalizing lessons[6].
- Positive self-talk boost self-confidence and self esteem[7]
- In a study conducted Roland Bénabou and Jean Tirole, self-confidence, which can be a byproduct of positive self-talk, was associated with enhanced motivation, more will power, and higher productivity[8]

Hearing positive ideas expressed about you is powerful, motivating, and good for mental and emotional health whether those positive ideas come from a loved one, a friend, a stranger, or you talking to yourself in the mirror. The only difference between the options is the last option is the one that should matter most to you and is the only potential source of appreciation that you can control. Turning on appreciation from the last option – yourself – creates an unlimited supply of emotional support.

If you don't consistently give yourself the appreciation and the love you need to exist at your best, then it's unreasonable to expect it from anyone else. At the same time, being appreciated is something that is beneficial and well within your control, so take the opportunity to supply yourself with this much needed positive stimuli.

WHY WE ARE CREATING A HABIT OF SELF APPRECIATION

Creating the habit of self appreciation and positive self-talk creates a limitless source of genuine and self-esteem boosting positivity without any reliance on external sources.

The resulting self-confidence increases the speed and intensity in which our tasks (and any positive task) become a habit. Thus, practicing self-appreciation every morning helps us ingrain our 10 daily tasks as habits sooner and more effectively learn from the realizations we'll have in the 75 day challenge.

Beyond our 75 days, self-appreciation remains an excellent form of emotional hygiene that, just like practicing thankfulness, contributes to good mental health.

In addition to your morning self-talk, here are a few ways you can appreciate yourself:

1. Remind yourself that the way you are exercising and eating healthily is the right thing, you're proud of yourself for doing it, and to keep doing it.
2. Remind yourself you're better than you were yesterday, and there's no need to compare yourself to anyone besides who you were yesterday.
3. Commend yourself for getting outside of your comfort zone.
4. Commend yourself on going through the slog of this 75 day challenge.
5. Commend yourself for trying something new.
6. Give yourself that compliment you deserve, and perhaps want, that no one has given.
7. Say anything else you'd love to hear.

We frequently receive feedback in daily life with most of it being critical. However, consider how often you are reminded of the positive things you do. How often are you reminded of the aspects of yourself and your efforts that you should maintain, reinforce, or double down on?

Nobody is perfect, and no one in this life will be. Solely focusing on imperfections to correct as the path to perfection is not only a dead-end effort but can also be life draining.

On the other hand, highlighting what is good, what is impressive, and what has been done well, then focusing on growing it is a much more energizing way to continually improve. Of course, you're never going to reach perfection, but this approach will bring you closer to the best version of you in a less soul-sucking way.

Let's take our garden metaphor from the thankfulness activity and apply it to our character and character traits.

Imagine if a garden, half full of useless weeds and plants we hate, and half great plants with delicious fruits that we love.

Imagine if, instead of pulling the weeds to improve our garden (which is miserable), we simply watered the fruiting plants. Imagine we gave our plants of choice some extra sunshine, so much that they grew over and overshadowed the plants we disliked. We'd achieve the same general result, a better garden, with a more enjoyable experience. Of course, it's still an imperfect garden, but it's better. Continually better.

We can treat ourselves and the traits that comprise us the same way.

Many people waste mental energy doubting who they are, instead of accepting and embracing who they are. Instead of embracing our natural strengths, like the power of being an introvert, the potential value of looking a little different from the crowd, or the potential strength in having a different perspective from most, we all too commonly obsess over our perceived faults that aren't even necessarily faults. At best, some people waste energy covering up what or who they are. At worst, they fight who they are, pretending that which makes them unique doesn't exist. In both cases, we are quite literally wasting mental energy holding ourselves back. We could be using that energy to harness the power of the thing that makes us different, unique, and is actually our advantage.

That's what this exercise is about; highlighting the things that we enjoy about ourselves and want to keep going, regardless of external circumstances. Highlighting these elements of ourselves that are strengths but go unseen at best and are misunderstood at worst then giving them the credit that is due. Here, via self-appreciation, give yourself credit for the potential and the regular achievements that no one else sees or acknowledges.

This approach is strategic. It is more efficient to build our strengths than it is to correct our weaknesses. This daily practice puts mental focus and appreciation on our strengths as the first step in increasing our strengths.

You should be the one person you can always rely on for love and support. You should be the one person whose company you enjoy the most. If you can achieve that, you will never be alone, you will always be loved, and you will always be appreciated. The first step on this path is appreciating who you are, strengths, flaws, and everything in between. That kind of self maintenance produces more strength than most people realize.

You aren't perfect, and you never will be. That doesn't mean those strengths and unique quirks should go unappreciated. If no one else knows, and if no one else appreciates them, you should embrace and appreciate them. As long as you're comfortable with them, you should grow them.

Just like with gratefulness, the things you put focus on will fill your vision, and in this case, boost confidence. The things you give attention and energy to will grow.

Take the initiative and appreciate yourself.

TAKEAWAYS ON SELF APPRECIATION
- If you make a habit of intentionally appreciating and supporting yourself, you will always have the support you need

DAILY TASK #3: BE STILL

How: Take 15 minutes of silence and stillness. Ideally, you'll spend this time meditating, but 15 minutes of just sitting consciously, and awake, aiming to relax, clear your mind, and just let whatever is going on go on is a solid mental reset.

THE SCIENCE AND BENEFITS OF MAKING TIME FOR STILLNESS

- Meditation has been shown in clinical research to be as effective as more "traditional" treatments against anxiety and depression.
- The positive effects on the brain of meditating have been shown in MRIs to remain after meditation is stopped, making the act of meditating beneficial far beyond the actual act of meditating[9]
- Clinical studies have shown meditation positively changes the expression of genes that regulate circadian rhythms, inflammation, and metabolism[10]

WHY ARE WE MEDITATING DURING THIS CHALLENGE?

- Meditation trains self-discipline and focus
- Meditation is an excellent form of mental hygiene that allows us to mentally "reset," withdrawing from the day and releasing as much mental weight and baggage as possible. This empty space of time allows us to return, and assess, with a fresh perspective.
- Studies show meditation benefits the body by relieving stress, anxiety, and worry related issues resulting in mental benefit as well as physical benefits.

MAKING TIME FOR STILLNESS IN OUR 75 DAY CHALLENGE

The **mind needs to be trained just like the body**, pushed to its limits and developed through intentional training.

However, for our bodies, we generally have very thorough training, recovery, and fueling methods. For a 45-minute training session, we may take a day off, eat specific foods to recover, stretch, etc.

But what about our minds?

For most people, the mind starts with a 9 to 10-hour workday, then moves to a few more hours wandering social media wherein our brains aren't quite positively engaged but can't turn off. That is in addition to anxiously obsessing about countless things throughout the day. We then retire to a night of sleep that carries with it all of the tensions, anxieties, and frustration from the day that are actually beyond our control, so worrying does no good. Then we awake and put our brains to work again, repeating the cycle.

But we need to remember, **just like the body, the mind needs to rest and recover.**

THE POINT: MENTAL RECOVERY NEEDS TO BE INTENTIONAL

Most of us don't intentionally schedule recovery time for our minds. We need time for our minds to pause and reset while we're awake to perform optimally. We need time to allow our mind to slow down. We need time to allow our minds to recover. To fix that, we're intentionally adding "stillness" to our day.

Adding the mental recovery and training component of stillness, quiet time, and meditation levels up our challenge. Now, we're not just challenging our mind with learning and discomfort. We're also promoting recovery from the mental as well as the physical standpoints, something many people overlook in their lives.

This intentional mental recovery helps us improve focus and mental strength by recharging our minds, just like a recovery day from the gym repairs our bodies.

Meditation, or just simply sitting in a hammock in silence lightly focused yet releasing thoughts and worries and anxieties, carves out time to build mental strength through the self-discipline of the rehabilitative practice of keeping the mind clear and being still.

By getting used to and actively achieving a still, calm mind we reprogram our baseline so that we can (at will) return to that calm, collected mental state, regardless of what happens around us.

No matter what your goals, 15 minutes of silence or meditation per day will do wonders for your mind

HERE'S A SIMPLE MEDITATION EXERCISE I RECOMMEND: BREATHE, FEEL, CLEAR

This simple, functional meditation exercise consists of three parts, five minutes each.

1. Find a place to relax and sit or lay down. Close your eyes.
2. For the first five minutes, relax and pay attention to your *natural* breath. Follow it in. Follow it out. Feel it. That's it.
3. For the second five minutes, mentally scan and feel your body. Start at your toes, aiming to feel *each* toe, then your foot, then move your awareness up to your ankles slowly, and continue through each part of your body until you reach your head. If you have time left, continue in reverse.
4. For the third part, just sit there, or lay there, with a clear mind and no activity. Relax. Don't pay attention to anything. Any thoughts that come, just relax and let them go.

That's it. A 15-minute rudimentary meditation exercise.

If you want a little light instruction and a lot of interesting information on meditation, I recommend Jon Kabat Zinn's book, *Wherever You Go, There You Are*

Additionally, I've found the Headspace app to be an excellent introduction and light training in meditation, mindfulness, and stillness.

If meditating is too "woo-woo," just give yourself 15 minutes to calm down and be alone with no stress or stimuli. No planning. No phone. No social media. Just sit. Just be.

FAQ: Do I have to Meditate?

No, you don't have to meditate. Any 15 minutes of conscious, quiet time, wherein your brain isn't focused on anything works. Browsing social media, watching tv, and chatting do not count, because your brain is still engaged. We want 15 minutes in which your brain is simply free.

FAQ: Can I use ambient noise, like rain or forest noises?

Use whatever makes your "stillness" time more relaxing.

Some schools of thought/meditation are very strict on how to meditate and dictate no ambient noise is allowed. However, the goal of *our* 15 minutes isn't for your to reach Nirvana or become a monk. We are simply creating an opportunity for your brain to rest, for you to relax and calm down, for your stress hormones to dip, and for you to ground yourself in a calm place.

TAKEAWAYS ON MEDITATION AND STILLNESS
- The mind needs to rest and actively recover just like the body. Meditation and stillness deliver that opportunity
- Meditation, and training the patience and focus to relax in aware stillness, trains mental discipline, ultimately building mental strength.
- Meditation has been shown through clinical research studies to positively affect the body's metabolism, inflammation, and (circadian) rhythm.

DAILY TASK #4: MOVE AND MOBILIZE

"Make time for fitness or make time for sickness."

How: Move or actively help your body recover every day. Exercise for two days, then take one day off to stretch and actively recover. Then, repeat. Aim for 45 minutes of movement in each exercise session.

For 75 days, we'll program consistent and balanced "movement" into our lives. Two days of exercise followed by one day of stretching and recovery to balance between exercise and recovery.

THE SCIENCE AND BENEFITS OF EXERCISING 2 DAYS, RESTING 1 DAY, AND REPEATING

- **Physical Benefits:** Individuals who exercise show a 72% lower risk of premature mortality from all causes compared with inactive individuals[11]
- **Mental Benefits:** Research studies have proven long term exercise improves mood and corelates with decreased likelihood of depression, while short term and long-term exercise improve cognitive performance
- Moderate intensity exercise has been associated with increased performance in working memory and cognitive flexibility, while high-intensity exercise

- **Emotional Benefits:** A Large-scale study of more than 1.2 million Americans found that people who exercised reported 43% fewer days of poor mental health in the past month than those who didn't exercise[13]
- **Recover:** Research into resistance trained individuals shows 48 hours to 72 as the optimal period for recovery per resistance trained muscle group to fully regain performance capability and realize exercise induced improvements.[14]

The bottom line is that science *proves* a long-term exercise habit improves quality of life and longevity physically, mentally, and emotionally.

The goal of this task isn't to get ripped or shed 10 pounds by day 75. The goal of this task is to build a habit of movement, any movement, balanced with intentional recovery by day 75. If you build in a routine, a desire, to either move and use your body or promote recovery every day, then you'll be better off in 75 days, a year, or 10 years from now.

The aggregate benefit of exercising, burning calories, and improving much needed mobility consistently over a year will add up to tremendous benefits including cardiovascular improvement, lower stress levels, and the practical strength that prevents injury. So, we want to design our training and plan for it to last not just 75 days, but instead beyond 75 days and ideally a lifetime.

By having an exercise plan of "2 on 1 off" - 2 days of exercise and one day of rest and stretching (mobility) and repeating we have the stimuli to improve physically (exercise). Then, we set aside time to recover while eating right, and give attention to active recovery. Remember, rest and recovery are essential parts of a healthy fitness plan. The second component rebuilds the mobility and flexibility many of us have lost in a lifetime of neglect.

ASSESSING FITNESS

The concept of "fitness" and a healthy body have gotten muddied in recent times, constantly mixing the practical elements – strength, stamina, and mobility – with popular opinions on the optimal aesthetics for the human body – a thin physique and visible abdominal muscles. To avoid confusion about our objectives for these 75 days in terms of fitness, let's get clear about what "fitness" truly is.

A good level of fitness should ultimately empower you to live the life want, uninhibited by physical ability (or a lack thereof) or risking injury.

For the purposes of simplicity and our goals, let's assess fitness as a combination of cardiovascular health and capability (or stamina), physical strength, and mobility (flexibility and strength through the entire range of motion of a joint). Now, let's assess how we can move (exercise) and recover with the goal of improving and maintaining cardiovascular health, strength, and mobility.

CARDIOVASCULAR FITNESS

The cardiovascular system and cardiopulmonary systems, consisting mainly of the heart, blood circulatory system, and lungs, is our system for getting nutrients to the muscles – so work can be performed – and taking waste from the muscles after work is completed, then repeating. The main mover, and the main muscle we want to condition in this process is the heart. The stronger and healthier your heart is, the more capable your heart is of pumping maximum blood with minimal effort and the easier it is for your heart to deliver more nutrients to your muscles and carry waste away during activity with minimal effort. This efficiency of the cardiovascular system at its best adds up to the ability to perform work steadily of increasingly longer periods of time and increasingly higher intensity while recovering quickly.

This cardiovascular health, and subsequent stamina, contributes to a higher quality of life. More stamina means more time to enjoy your favorite sport before feeling winded, more capability to play with and keep up with your children, better sexual performance, and even improved mental focus thanks to healthier blood flow to the brain.

HOW TO IMPROVE YOUR CARDIOVASCULAR HEALTH OVER THE NEXT 75 DAYS

The best pathway to a healthy heart, for a person with no existing health issues, is to simply *use* your heart. Daily, do something that gets your heart pumping and just keep going. Any movement is better than no movement. You don't need a gym, you don't need a rowing machine, and you don't need a treadmill. Instead, walking or running in the park, taking on a game of basketball or a soccer match, or playing with your kids at full speed is sufficient cardiovascular exercise as long as your heart is pumping at a high enough rate (beats per minute) to be considered exercise.

According to the CDC, moderately exercising 150 minutes per week (at 64% to 76% of your max heart rate) or 75 minutes per week of vigorous exercise (77% to 93% of your max heartrate) is the recommended minimum for cardiovascular health[15],[16],[17].

To calculate your maximum heart rate apply the formula 220 – [your age] = your maximum heartrate.

Age	Maximum Heart	Moderate Heart Rate			Vigorous Heart Rate		
		64%	to	76%	77%	to	93%
18	202	129	to	154	156	to	188
19	201	129	to	153	155	to	187
20	200	128	to	152	154	to	186
21	199	127	to	151	153	to	185
22	198	127	to	150	152	to	184
23	197	126	to	150	152	to	183
24	196	125	to	149	151	to	182
25	195	125	to	148	150	to	181
26	194	124	to	147	149	to	180
27	193	124	to	147	149	to	179
28	192	123	to	146	148	to	179
29	191	122	to	145	147	to	178
30	190	122	to	144	146	to	177
31	189	121	to	144	146	to	176
32	188	120	to	143	145	to	175
33	187	120	to	142	144	to	174
34	186	119	to	141	143	to	173
35	185	118	to	141	142	to	172
36	184	118	to	140	142	to	171
37	183	117	to	139	141	to	170
38	182	116	to	138	140	to	169
39	181	116	to	138	139	to	168
40	180	115	to	137	139	to	167
41	179	115	to	136	138	to	166
42	178	114	to	135	137	to	166
43	177	113	to	135	136	to	165
44	176	113	to	134	136	to	164
45	175	112	to	133	135	to	163
46	174	111	to	132	134	to	162
47	173	111	to	131	133	to	161
48	172	110	to	131	132	to	160
49	171	109	to	130	132	to	159

Chart produced in accordance with Physical Activity Guidelines Advisory Committee report guidelines (Physical Activity Guidelines Advisory Committee Report, 2008. Washington, DC: U.S. Dept of Health and Human Services; 2008)

Age	Maximum Heart	Moderate Heart Rate			Vigorous Heart Rate		
		64%	to	76%	77%	to	93%
50	170	109	to	129	131	to	158
51	169	108	to	128	130	to	157
52	168	108	to	128	129	to	156
53	167	107	to	127	129	to	155
54	166	106	to	126	128	to	154
55	165	106	to	125	127	to	153
56	164	105	to	125	126	to	153
57	163	104	to	124	126	to	152
58	162	104	to	123	125	to	151
59	161	103	to	122	124	to	150
60	160	102	to	122	123	to	149
61	159	102	to	121	122	to	148
62	158	101	to	120	122	to	147
63	157	100	to	119	121	to	146
64	156	100	to	119	120	to	145
65	155	99	to	118	119	to	144
66	154	99	to	117	119	to	143
67	153	98	to	116	118	to	142
68	152	97	to	116	117	to	141
69	151	97	to	115	116	to	140
70	150	96	to	114	116	to	140
71	149	95	to	113	115	to	139
72	148	95	to	112	114	to	138
73	147	94	to	112	113	to	137
74	146	93	to	111	112	to	136
75	145	93	to	110	112	to	135
76	144	92	to	109	111	to	134
77	143	92	to	109	110	to	133
78	142	91	to	108	109	to	132
79	141	90	to	107	109	to	131
80	140	90	to	106	108	to	130

Chart produced in accordance with Physical Activity Guidelines Advisory Committee report guidelines (Physical Activity Guidelines Advisory Committee Report, 2008. Washington, DC: U.S. Dept of Health and Human Services; 2008)

By the CDC recommendations, light jogging or moderate exercise 5 x 30 minutes per week, such as walking or jogging, or intense exercise 5 x 75 minutes per week, like wind sprints or functional weightlifting, is just enough for solid heart health.

Note that you can split this time (150 minutes of moderate intensity exercise or 75 minutes of vigorous exercise per week) any way you want and still achieve the results we want. As long as your heart rate gets going and stays going, biking to work counts, playing rugby counts, and sex counts for your daily exercise as well.

STRENGTH

Physical strength is the ability to move ourselves or move an object and is a practical necessity for normal activity in everyday life for self-sufficiency, for injury resistance, for longevity and for a high quality of life in old age.

Walking in old age is only possible with an adequately strong posterior chain (glutes, lower back and the smaller muscle groups between and around). Doing chores on a daily basis, such as carrying groceries, a book bag, or a child, are easier and less likely to end in usage injuries if we have functional strength. Injury resistance in the case of an accident, a fall, or a wrong move during sports is made possible by having the strength to adequately control your movements, in both starting and stopping.

Functional strength improves our quality of life and should be an element of every well-balanced fitness program.

HOW TO TRAIN FOR FUNCTIONAL STRENGTH IN YOUR 75 DAY CHALLENGE

At a minimum of twice weekly, exercise with some form

of resistance to train functional, full body strength or train strength each individual part of the body for strength twice weekly. Whether bodyweight/calisthenics, free weights, sandbags, kettlebells, or suspension training, use some tool and protocol to train for strength in all planes of movement of your upper body, lower body, and core.

For those in need of more information on training for functional strength, consider these resources.

- Weightlifting and Mobility: "Becoming a Supple Leopard: The Ultimate Guide to Resolving Pain, Preventing Injury, and Optimizing Athletic Performance" by Kelly Starrett
- Functional Fitness: The free daily workout at Crossfit.com accompanied by the free Crossfit Level I trainer handbook, downloadable at Crossfit.com
- Calisthenics: "Overcoming Gravity: A Systematic Approach to Gymnastics and Bodyweight Strength" by Steven Low
- Suspension Training: Use the free training resources available through TRX and Monkii

You can find links to these sites and resources on the constantly updated list at ABrotherAbroad.com/75-Strong-Resources

HOW TO MOVE FOR BETTER STAMINA, STRENGTH, AND MOBILITY IN YOUR 75 DAY CHALLENGE

For the "movement" portion, either aim for 20 to 30 minutes of high-intensity exercise with a minimum of 15 minutes of intense activity (i.e., Crossfit, kettlebell training, Tabata, circuit training, and resistance training with less than 60 seconds rest between sets) or 45 minutes of any activity you choose that gets your heart pumping moderately with a minimum of 30 minutes of moderate activity.

Though resistance training and HIIT workouts bear the most benefit, any healthy movement is good movement.

Whatever structure and schedule you choose, the CDC recommends a minimum of 150 minutes of moderate activity per week or 75 minutes of vigorous activity split any way you'd like.

If you want to walk the dog for 45 minutes, walk. If you want to hike, go hike. If you want to shoot some hoops then hit the court and go hard for 45 minutes.

High-intensity interval training will burn the most fat and will have the best cardio benefits. Research has shown that while moderate intensity exercise, like cardio centric running, burns calories during the exercise, high intensity training (HIIT) burns calories during exercise and keeps your metabolism elevated for up to 48 hours after you finish[18].

However, **simply building a long-term habit of moving daily is more valuable than pounds lost in the short term or doing a specific workout for 75 days.**

If you need high-intensity workout inspiration you can do without a gym, I recommend these options:

- The 10,000 kettlebell swing challenge
- These Sandbag HIIT workouts you can do at home; all you need is a solid sandbag with handles

- These Crossfit workouts you can do at home
- The free "30 Days of Yoga with Adrienne" series on YouTube
- Alternate between the Crossfit "Murph" hero workout, 250 kettlebell swings, and the JT hero workout. (These workouts are listed at the end of this book)
- The ABA Fitness page (ABrotherAbroad.com/Fitness) has plenty of workouts and fitness ideas for staying in shape anywhere

REST AFTER TWO DAYS OF EXERCISE

Research into resistance trained individuals shows 48 hours to 72 as the optimal period for recovery per resistance trained muscle group to fully regain performance capability and realize exercise induced improvements.[19]

This means that every two days that we move and exercise should be balanced with one day of "active rest." On these days you'll skip the workout, and you'll do relaxing but beneficial stretching instead. "2 on 1 off."

By training or exercising especially at high intensity, we create the conditions for physical improvement – slight but beneficial tissue damage takes place, the hormone profile in our body shifts to better repair the damaged tissue, our metabolic processes increase and use the food we've eaten differently to repair damaged tissue - but that physical improvement happens in our recovery periods. That recovery cannot happen during exercise, and requires a full 24 to 72 hours to take place depending on diet, the individual, and exercise intensity. Recovery is essential to progressing physically and avoiding injury. If you are engaging in an intense fitness program, I recommend two days of working out and one day off. Five days on and two days off is also an option for lower intensity resistance programs or programs that intensely train each bodypart only once per week or only at moderate intensity.

For any effective fitness regimen, you need rest. In an adequately intense fitness program, two days of exercise creates the right amount of stimuli (tissue damage, hormone production) to make good use of a day of recovery, helping us build strength and burn fat optimally. Over the 75 days, our goal isn't destruction. Our goal is strength, stamina, and mobility gains, and creating habits that support that in the long run.

This potential habit, training for two days, resting one, and getting back to training the following day, is a routine we can and should do into old age and indefinitely. If this challenge programs in that routine, you've won.

For rest days, set a timer for 20 minutes and just stretch each of your trouble spots aiming for 1-minute minimum and 2 minutes optimally per direction of movement/rotation at each joint targeting the hips, quads, hamstring, calves, shoulders, chest, forearms via the, and additionally targeting the whole posterior chain. Then check your box on the challenge checklist for that day.

TAKEAWAYS ON MOVING AND MOBILIZING

- Exercise reduces your risk of early death, improves cognitive performance, and correlates with a lower occurrence of depression and sadness
- Workout for two days, then rest and recover one day focusing on stretching. Alternatively, exercise five days, then rest for two days. DO NOT skip rest days altogether
- Any movement is good movement, as long as you get your heart rate to minimum 64% of your maximum heart rate
- Aim for a minimum total of 75 minutes per week of

mid to high intensity exercise (min. 77% of max heart rate) or 150 minutes per week of moderate exercise (minimum 64% of your max heart rate). That equates 15 mins x 5 days or 30 mins x 5 days per week respectively.
- On rest days, stretch and mobilize aiming to stretch and extended the range of motion of every joint as well as the strength throughout the range of motion, for injury proofing and longevity

DAILY TASK #5: EAT HEALTHY

How: Follow these healthy eating guidelines

- Eat meat and vegetables, nuts and seeds, some fruit
- Keep intake to levels that will support exercise but not body fat
- Eliminate processed sugar
- Minimize refined carbohydrates (bread, cakes, pasta, etc.)
- Consider applying an 8 to 12 hour eating window (intermittent fasting) with the permission of your doctor.
- Add nutrient-dense food (high in vitamins, minerals, antioxidants, and beneficial bioactive compounds) to every meal.

Following these eating guidelines will, in the long term, lead to healthy body weight, lower risk of disease, and deliver the nutrition necessary for optimal physical performance.

THE SCIENCE OF TOO MUCH SUGAR: UNCONTROLLABLE APPETITE, CHRONIC INFLAMMATION, HIGH BLOOD PRESSURE, AND FATTY LIVER DISEASE

- According to the National Cancer Institute, the **average American male consumes 24 teaspoons of added sugar, an additional 384 calories per day**
- The **American Heart Association suggests that men consume no more than 150 calories** (about 9 teaspoons or 36 grams) per day, or a single 12oz. can of soda, as the upper limit
- **Excess Sugar Causes Uncontrollable Appetite and Weight Gain:** Excess consumption of sugar turns of the appetite control system in the body, making you feel like you're still hungry after eating, resulting in consumption of surplus calories and ultimately weight gain
- **Sugar Increases Risk of Heart Attack and Stroke:** All of the major side effects of consuming sugar - higher blood pressure, inflammation, weight gain, diabetes, and fatty liver disease – are linked to increased risk of heart attack and stroke
- Source: Harvard Health[20]

THE SCIENCE AND BENEFITS OF INTERMITTENT FASTING

- Intermittent fasting has been proven in clinical research to improve cardiometabolic health via lowering blood pressure and oxidative stress, lowering the desire to eat and increasing insulin sensitivity. These benefits occur whether or not weight loss occurs.[21]

Food is fuel for your body. Put in clean fuel that allows the system (your body) to function with as few harmful byproducts as possible, and the system will perform at its best and last longer. In the human body, that translates to better performance with a lower risk of disease over a longer lifetime.

Eating "healthy" is simply eating with a set of habits that reduce the risk of disease and enable your body to perform at its best from strength, stamina, and cardiovascular standpoint.

AVOID DIETS!

In this day and age, a new fad diet hits the internet every .5 seconds and infects the population with hearsay while delivering minimal scientific backing, if any. We want to avoid unproven or unfounded ideas as there is no guarantee that the diet serves our general goal – better performance and lower risk of disease – and may actually carry many risks to our health and goals.

When it comes to diets, only listen to three people: your doctor, your licensed nutritionist, and yourself. Rely on the opinion of the last person the most. Be open to science backed ideas for healthy eating, and be skeptical of loosely recommended diets.

Many popular "diets" are actually strict eat regimens intended to treat medical conditions, not intended to support a healthy average lifestyle for healthy individuals.

Additionally, many fad diets are aimed solely at burning fat. They're not intended to provide a healthy way to fuel an active lifestyle of exercise, exploration, and contentment. Don't eat for the body you want; eat for the life you want to live.

"Dieting," is often a detrimental and at worst risky and often worthless pursuit in the long term. For most people, diets consist of a very artificial set of eating habits followed with the sole goal of losing a few pounds. Often, once that goal is achieved, the routines that supported the new body weight are ditched. Eating habits then return to a level that provides "surplus calories" that are stored by the body. Eventually, the pounds are regained, and we're back where we started - making the diet worthless in the long term.

This is the main reason "diets" aren't something we want to pursue. They're unsustainable. The "habits" in diets such as keto, the Mediterranean diet, and the zone diet, etc. can't be maintained in the long term while keeping our sanity and staying healthy.

What we want is to program in sustainable eating habits that fuel us to perform, keep our weight at a healthy level, that leave us feeling good, and that we could do indefinitely. Whatever eating habits we choose, we should be able to maintain them for decades while continually improving our bodies and maintaining healthy, optimal body weight.

What we want is to incorporate scientifically-backed healthy eating habits that 1) we are certain generally improve our health (based on scientific research and years of testing) 2) we can maintain and stay healthy well after the 75 days.

I highly recommend considering these eating guidelines. Ask your doctor about practicing the following eating habits over the next 75 days:

1. Eat meat and vegetables, nuts and seeds, and some fruit
2. Skip refined sugar as much as possible
3. Skip refined carbohydrates (bread, cakes, candy bars, etc.)
4. Eat a savory breakfast, heavy with proteins, healthy fats, and veggies, instead of a sugary breakfast.
5. Intentionally eat vegetables at every meal.

This is excellent advice for the average eater with no health issues. In the long term, your weight will drop to a healthy level, and you'll have enough fuel for the workouts and activities that make you feel alive.

Additionally, start your day with a protein, fat, and a veggie-heavy breakfast - not a sugar bomb coated with syrup or a sugary frappe. By doing this, you avoid negative sugar induced hormone spikes that at best lead to hunger spikes in the short and at worst promote obesity, cardiovascular disease, and countless other issues in the long term.

Be sure to calculate your basal metabolic rate, which is the number of calories your body needs to function properly, not accounting for exercise or extra activity. Then, using your basal metabolic rate, calculate the fat, protein, and carbohydrate maximums (in grams and calories) daily. Then, understand that unless you burn it off, any calories beyond your basal metabolic rate WILL stick to you – stored as fat.[22]

Last, I recommend considering adding an "eating window" or intermittent fasting – with the permission of your doctor. Maintaining an extended period each day wherein our stomachs stay empty has the following benefits:

- Helps us avoid excessive food-induced hormone spikes throughout the day that highly correlate with disease and inflammation, trigger hunger spikes and store more food eaten as fat
- Gives your body a period to burn off stored food (fat) while the stomach is empty instead of burning the food you've just eaten
- Gives your body a period wherein no energy is spent digesting food, leaving those metabolic resources for the immune systems/recovery systems to be fully engaged.

- Best of all, intermittent fasting is a habit that we can apply to our lives indefinitely and that will positively benefit us indefinitely.

The only exception to the "avoid diets" guideline that I recommend talking to your doctor about is the elimination diet.

The elimination diet is a 21-day eating protocol in which you only eat foods that are associated with low allergic reactions and low inflammation. During the 21-day period, you and abide by an 8 to 10 hour eating window intermittent fasting protocol.

For those 21 days, eating only these "clean" foods gives your body (and immune system) a chance to clean things up as you only eat easily digestible foods with minimal negative effects on the body – but this isn't the primary benefit of the elimination diet.

The primary benefit of the elimination diet comes after the 21-day diet ends when you add your old "normal foods" back to your diet one by one. The 21 days of clean eating creates a great baseline for your body, likely with less inflammation and fewer gut issues than most of us normally experience. Thus, as you add foods back, you'll be able to clearly correlate each food with its effects in your body. During this reintegration period, you pay attention to which foods improve how your body functions and which foods actually affect you negatively. You'll decipher exactly which foods are your power foods as well as which foods cause bloating, digest slowly, and leave you feeling lethargic or worse.

Every person and everybody have unique needs, sensitivities, and strengths. The elimination diet offers a structured scientific process for identifying the best and worst foods – and general eating guidelines – for you. Thus, allowing you to ditch "diets" for good in exchange for tailored, healthy eating guidelines for your body.

Keep in mind the elimination diet is NOT intended to lose weight. I consider the elimination diet more of an educational experience for you about your body. As a side effect, you will experience less inflammation generally and in your digestive tract, less bloating, etc. Having a six-pack make an appearance is another potential side effect, but that shouldn't be the aim.

Every few years, I run through the elimination diet eating protocol as a check-up and reset. Each time, at the end of the diet, I find my appetite and taste preferences pleasantly reset toward healthier foods (nutrient-dense, non-fried, non-starchy) and any gut issues (traveler stomach, Bali belly) clear up.

Note: This information is shared as a perspective on nutrition and eating practices that have benefited me and my clients in the past. I recommend researching any nutrition changes for yourself and discussing them with your doctor or licensed nutritionist or dietician before trying an elimination diet.

HOW TO BUILD THESE HEALTHY EATING GUIDELINES INTO YOUR 75-DAY PROGRAM

Pick three healthy eating guidelines and stick with them through the challenge.

For example:
1. No added sugar
2. A vegetable with every meal
3. No eating after 6pm or before 8am

Though this approach doesn't eliminate *everything* bad, it's good because it starts us on the right track of building healthy eating habits in a manageable way. Additionally, in comparison to the benefits of a "start and stop" diet, which only lasts for a few weeks with most people, the aggregate benefit of even one of these small changes over a lifetime is very significant.

For my challenge, I chose and recommend the following three eating guidelines.

1. Intermittent fasting with an 8-hour eating window
2. Eliminating refined sugar
3. Limiting refined carbs (bread) to one meal every few days

These changes alone were enough to see pounds drop, feel an energy boost, and feel general improvement over 75 days without the eating guidelines being unsustainable. I've also decided to maintain these eating habits indefinitely.

TAKEAWAYS ON EATING IN THE 75 DAY CHALLENGE

- Skip added sugar and refined sugars, as this is arguably the single biggest eating related step you can take for a healthier body
- Calculate your basal metabolic calorie rate, and your daily protein, fats, and carbs
- Become familiar with the calorie content per serving, and size of a serving, for the 10 foods you eat the most
- Consider applying an 8 to 12 hour eating window to reduce inflammation and give your body a window of time when it isn't digesting.
- Don't do diets

- Do abide by specific healthy eating guidelines tailored for your body and lifestyle

DAILY TASK #6: SKIP ALCOHOL

How: Just don't drink alcohol at all. Simple as that

Anything that, by nature, reduces performance is worth skipping *if* your goal is a better life.

As accepted as alcohol is in society, it has a massive list of side effects that make it questionable when consumed in moderation and definitely detrimental in excess.

THE SCIENCE OF DRINKING ALCOHOL AND WHY TO AVOID IT

1. Any amount of alcohol causes irreversible brain damage and there is no safe level of alcohol consumption in terms of brain health[23]. Anything that causes brain damage is worth skipping.

2. Alcohol negatively affects sleep cycles, which reduces mental performance, and increases risk of heart disease and countless other diseases, in addition to leading to emotional volatility for the following days.

3. Alcohol reduces cardiovascular performance by roughly 11% after heavy consumption[24].

4. Alcohol abuse (more than 14 drinks per week) leads to liver damage that *can* be reversed if recognized early and if the drinker stops drinking completely[25]. One more reason to skip for 75 days.

5. Alcohol is commonly and unknowingly used as a coping mechanism to deal with discomfort – internally or externally. This robs us of the opportunity to fully understand, deal with, solve, and grow from the difficulties in front of us.

6. Alcohol consumption reduces the function and efficiency of your immune system

All of our reasons for skipping alcohol during this challenge are either to avoid permanent damage to our bodies or to reverse the damage we've already done to our bodies.

These 75 days without alcohol will allow you to regain a clear head, level your emotions, and reach peak physical performance.

Additionally, you can use these 75 days to recalibrate your relationship with alcohol. Because of how accepted and commonly consumed as alcohol is in society, the average person is very unlikely to abstain from alcohol indefinitely. However, we can recalibrate our relationship with alcohol. Drinking more than 14 drinks per week (2 to 3 standard drinks per night) or drinking to relax and calm down (a common coping mechanism) are more common occurrences than most people think. By completely eliminating alcohol from our lives for a period, we break the small habits and unintentional relationship we have *may* have with alcohol. After 75 days, when we reintroduce alcohol, we will do so with clearer intentions and recalibrated expectations and limits.

You have nothing to lose by skipping alcohol, and most people have a lot to gain.

Our greatest strength lies in performing at our best without aids or hindrances. We'll skip alcohol for the next 75 days to get back in touch with our "uninfluenced selves" and give our livers a rest.

DAILY TASK #7: READ FOR 15 MINUTES

How: Spend 15 minutes reading a book or listening to an audiobook daily, fiction or non-fiction. No blogs, no social media.

Our goal: Build a habit of reading for the benefit of intentionally absorbing well researched knowledge and continually training the brain in the areas of memory, comprehension, and critical analysis. Additionally, by reading we train our abilities to empathize, which is a specific outcome of reading fiction. This 15 minutes per day of reading is also aimed to balance the negative effects that can come from an information diet of purely social media sourced, short form content, and shared thoughts with thin, unsubstantiated ideas.

THE SCIENCE AND BENEFITS OF READING: MORE EMPATHY, LOWER STRESS, BETTER MEMORY AND CRITICAL THINKING, AND PRINT IS BETTER THAN DIGITAL

- Reading daily is proven in clinical studies to drastically improve memory, critical thinking, the ability to concentrate, the ability to handle stress, and memory
- Research shows that people who regularly read fiction show a heightened ability to empathize and understand the feelings and beliefs of others[26]

- 30 minutes of reading lowered blood pressure, heart rate, and feelings of psychological distress just as much as yoga or humor in a study on reading and stress[27]
- A study comparing the value of reading print versus reading on digital formats found higher comprehension and recall with print (book or newspaper) over digital formats[28]
- Researchers found that listening to audiobooks or reading print books led to the same level of comprehension and knowledge retention[29]

Cracking open a nice, long, thought-provoking book (or sliding through one on an e-reader) challenges our brains and expands our minds without relying on the addictive hormone response triggered by social media.

The process that then occurs, relative to scrolling on social media, is significantly more favorable.

Simply opening a book, reading, absorbing and critiquing ideas presented over tens or hundreds of pages exercises and enriches your mind without the sensationalism and playing up to emotions that happen on social media.

Reading for 15 minutes per day gets us back into the habit of intentionally choosing what we learn and absorb (instead of having it suggested) and committing to drinking in complex ideas made up of complex ideas over chapters and volumes.

Additionally, choosing to read a non-fiction book gives us the opportunity to consciously expose ourselves to ideas that, at first glance, don't align with our own but can cause perspective shifts – ultimately expanding our own sphere of ideas and awareness.

"Reading daily is proven in clinical studies to drastically improve memory, critical thinking, the ability to concentrate, the ability to handle stress, and memory..."

Reading is the equivalent of a mental workout that not only trains our cognitive processes – memory, critical analysis, focus and concentration – but has also been correlated in research with lower likelihood of dementia and Alzheimer's. Just as we are doing with our body, through exercise, and passively with our mind, through meditation, the active process of reading helps us train, grow, and maintain our cognitive abilities

"Research shows that people who regularly read fiction show a heightened ability to empathize and understand the feelings and beliefs of others"[30]

Whether non-fiction or fiction, the books we read have thorough benefits. Emotional intelligence, the capacity to be aware of, control, and express one's emotions, and to handle interpersonal relationships judiciously and empathetically is a valued capability in the corporate world, in raising children, and even in successful relationships. The empathy and emotion derived capability strength that comes from understanding other is something we could all use more of. Understanding people, whether they're on your side or on a side you're negotiating with, is a valuable strength and reading fiction gives you more of that strength

"Reading lowered blood pressure, heart rate, and feelings of psychological distress just as much as yoga or humor in another study"[31]

The average person in today's world has plenty of things to stress about. This task – reading – is proven to *remove* that stress more as you complete it.

"A study comparing the value of reading print versus reading on digital formats found higher comprehension and recall with print (book or newspaper) over digital formats"[32]

Use this task as an opportunity to put down the devices, because your good old paperback book is more conducive to learning, comprehending, absorbing, and recalling what you read.

Take back the opportunity to intentionally read words of your choosing and absorb information for mental enrichment.

Consciously choose education over entertainment.

TAKEAWAYS ON COMMITTING TO READ 15 MINUTES DAILY

- Reading (or listening) to books gives us a chance to regain the mental fitness many of are losing in our social media and short form content dominated world.
- Even reading fiction carries the normal benefits of reading and trains your ability to accurately be aware of and understand other's emotions and beliefs
- Reading is proven to reduce stress
- Put down the cell phone or tablet and grab a normal book for maximum benefit

DAILY TASK #8: SPEND 15 MINUTES LEARNING A NEW SKILL

How: Spend 15 minutes per day learning something new or continuing to learn something

THE SCIENCE BEHIND LEARNING EVERY DAY

- Continually learning creates a healthier, more capable brain thanks to neuroplasticity. Though children benefit most heavily from opportunities to focus their attention, introduction to novel concepts, and challenges to stimulate positive changes in the brain, adults experience significant positive adaptions in the brain from learning as well.[33]

When we learn, we grow, and nothing is constant in human existence - we are constantly changing, never static. The moment we stop learning, we stop growing and start degrading.

All too often, we enter a job or station in life, and become comfy there. We gradually give up the pursuit of learning new abilities. If the world never changes, this isn't much of a problem. However, the world and the civilization we live in change at an increasingly fast pace.

If we don't evolve and adapt, we risk becoming obsolete or extinct, unable to perform in the "new world."

Even worse, by not expanding our skillset and knowledge set, we risk missing out on opportunities that pop up in an ever-changing world. We leave ourselves unequipped, lacking the right mental tools, skills, or abilities to capitalize on new opportunities as they show up.

By cultivating a "growth mindset" and continually learning something new, whether we need to use the new skill or not, we'll be prepared to seize novel opportunities that others can't.

Even if you don't know the necessary skill for the moment, if you are used to the act of learning, learning one more thing will be easier than it otherwise would be. The craving and hunger to learn will make the process of learning easier as well.

Each of us have so many things we would *love* to learn or do if we could flip a switch and skip the learning process.

So, go learn. Cook gourmet cuisine. Speak French. Throw a curveball. Paint a sunset. Rock Climb. Sing. Sculpt concrete. Anything. Just learn.

Even further, there are concepts we can learn that will improve our lives. From learning how to strive for a healthier relationship, to learning how to train a dog, to learning how to self-publish a book, we all have opportunities to learn *something* that could improve the quality of and possibilities in our lives.

Fortunately, we can't skip the learning process, and we get to experience the joy of learning something we want to. Not something required for our job. Not something required for our degree. Not something required by our parents, our culture, or our religion.

We get to experience the process of learning something *we want* to know.

Use this challenge as a catalyst to start learning something you want to do. Learn to blog. Learn to do comedy. Learn magic tricks.

For 15 minutes every day, hit YouTube, open a book, or simply practice to experience learning something you want to learn.

THE TAKEAWAYS ON LEARNING
- The more you aspire to learn, the easier learning becomes
- Building a habit of learning new skills creates a surplus of skills ready to seize unexpected opportunities

DAILY TASK #9: EXPRESS A PASSION

"Get busy living, or get busy dying."

How: Spend 15 minutes fully engaged in doing something that you're passionate about

THE SCIENCE AND BENEFITS OF DOING THINGS YOU ENJOY
- In a clinical study, enjoyable leisure activities, taken in the aggregate, were associated with higher and better psychosocial and physical measures relevant for health and well-being - lower blood pressure, total cortisol, waist circumference, body mass index, and perceptions of better physical function[34]
- Research shows taking a break[35] to do something we enjoy can weaken ingrained habits, routines, and modes of thinking that prevent progress while helping us discover new problem-solving approaches for work and life[36]

I won't try to hypothesize about the meaning of life, but I can talk all day about the opportunities of life.

Every day of your existence, life presents chances to think, feel, and experience. If you are not feeling or experiencing at least one thing you're passionate about at least once a day, you're wasting one of the most incredible opportunities in life – just enjoying it.

The passion, and experiencing it, don't have to be significant. It just needs to make you feel pure and simple pleasure.

For example:
- Play with your children
- Sit and talk with a loved one
- Dance in your room with the music cranked up
- Paint an indecipherable painting
- Play Anthony Bourdain and be a chef attempting to cook a gourmet meal at home while watching a food travel show
- Sing your lungs out for 15 minutes
- Do a woodworking project and build that bookshelf you need
- Read to your children
- Tell your kids about your childhood, or ask about theirs
- Do something that you are passionate about. Do anything else that excites you.

DAILY TASK #10: EMBRACE THE PROCESS

How: Keep a journal and check off every task you complete every day to consciously embrace and appreciate simply following through with the process. Additionally, share thoughts, ideas, and realizations in the journal as an emotional and mental stress release daily. Just doing what it takes every day to build a foundation of positive, lifelong habits is what embracing the process is about.

THE SCIENCE OF FOCUSING ON THE PROCESS INSTEAD OF THE RESULT

- Research studies have shown that focusing on the process, instead of the results or outcome, improves cognitive performance and learning of motor skills[37] and higher consistency between distant and near future decisions[38] which can be interpreted as more mental and emotional stability driving more consistent analytical and cognitive processes.

THE SCIENCE OF USING CHECKLISTS TO EMBRACE THE PROCESS

Whenever we complete a goal and experience the success of completing that goal our brains release dopamine as a reward. Dopamine is connected to positive feelings of pleasure and motivation, thus reinforcing the desire to do again what has been done – in this case, completing the task on our list and checking it off as acknowledgment. Thus, completing a task, such as the ones on our checklist, is a small goal completed, a small success, which in return receives a release of dopamine from your brain. By using this checklist and making the act of writing our checkmark in our list the figurative finish line for that goal, we are formalizing the act, recognizing completion of it, and reinforcing the desire and need to do that act again without regard to the results or outcome.

By using a checklist and leveraging how our brains function, releasing dopamine as a reward and motivation in response to a desirable act, we are embracing the act of the process and the tasks within to build positive habits.

THE SCIEND AND BENEFITS OF JOURNALING: IMPROVED MOOD AND MENTAL STATE

- In a 2006 study, adults were asked to spend 15 minutes per day journaling about a stressful event or writing about plans for the future, twice weekly. The group that journaled, compared to the control group, saw the largest reduction in symptoms of depression, anxiety, and hostility.
- Other studies[39],[40] associated journaling with an immune system boost and partially credited it to a process described as "emotional disclosure."

Fall in love with the process, and you'll never be disappointed by the result. You'll realize it's about something more significant.

We have become a society that thrives on instant gratification and instant everything. We're so used to instant meals, instant deliveries, and instant responses that (for most) when we don't see instant results, crippling and counterproductive anxiety starts banging at the door. These unreasonable expectations and accompanying anxiety then distract us from diligently focusing on the process that could create the results we really want.

The solution: fall in love with the process.

If we can make the primary goal and focus simply doing each step of the process as best we can at that moment, putting our entire focus on that step, and (if we're lucky) enjoying that diligent act, we don't need to worry about anything. Firstly, because we know we've given it our best, obsessing won't improve the result. Secondly, if we put our whole focus into the task in front of us, we can trust that, on average, the result will be stellar. We don't need to worry about the result. We can just focus on the process.

The popular 75-day challenges tasked participants with assignment to "take a picture a day" to "track progress." Although this could be a fun and exciting opportunity to, at a later date, revel in the progress we made, it could also be a mental trap.

We could easily get caught up examining the picture, and ourselves, the moment after we take it. We could get caught up comparing our picture from today to the pic from yesterday and the day before to see if we've improved. All the while obsessing over *if* we should have improved since then or if we improved enough.

That act, examining the result before we have fully completed the process would be a waste of focus and energy if we trust the process. This focus and energy could have been used to diligently perform our tasks and our process to better achieve the result we're after.

We want to fall in love with simply doing the process, disconnected from the short-term outcome. The short-term result isn't our goal; doing the process the best we can is our goal. That approach will deliver the best possible results as a simple byproduct.

Throughout the 75 days of this program, don't stare at your waistline. Don't question how much you've learned. Don't critique whether your singing has improved. That's not what this is about.

Instead, look at your journal and checklist. Look at the days and tasks you've checked off in this challenge as the only proof you need that you're doing the work and putting in the effort to make a stronger you. Every check-in every box is evidence that you are a stronger person than yesterday.

A stronger you. *That* is all we're after.

TAKEAWAYS
- Fall in love with the process
- Do not obsess over the results
- Keep a checklist to track your progress within the process of the 75 days
- Consider keeping a journal to record thoughts for reflection later

CHAPTER 6: ELITE MILITARY TRAINING AS A MODEL FOR DEVELOPMENT

During my time of service in the Marine Corps, I ran into a wide range of service members

There were the normal ones. They showed up and did a job that quite honestly was similar to something many people do in the "real world." They did their job and served honorably and went home.

Then there was a breed that was one step further. Warriors by ethos dedicated to a job that bordered on a calling that required toughness, reprogramming, and sacrifice. Grunts, hitters, and combat vets aplenty, all of them were trained and conditioned to be the dogs of war.

Last was a completely different breed, varied in job and origin, but always of exceptional caliber and quality. Many of them were "operators," shooters that had been honing their craft so long and so diligently that they seemed more like gods of war than well-trained mortals.

Everyone I knew in this last class of warriors was impressive and shared a few common traits. They were all calm, cool, and collected no matter what came their way. They were all intelligent and knowledgeable, confident, and ready. Always ready. Their missions varied so widely there wasn't a template – but something in them made none of that matter. Whatever the battle, they always won.

That last class of warriors, and how they reached that level of superhuman performance, is what the idea of this 75-day program is modeled on.

Within the US military, from my experience and observations, there is a separate set of advanced and elite military training beyond the basic training that reprograms those "selected." Over the course of their respective "pipelines" they internalize habits, tactics, and ways of existing that make them exponentially more effective than your average soldier, sailor, airmen, or Marine

However, there is a common misconception about many of these advanced and elite military training courses.

From the outside, the toughest schools in the military are reputed as simply ripping you apart. Though there definitely are some schools that take that approach – that is usually not so.

Elite military training is generally divided into two categories or stages. There is the kind that breaks you down to your core to test your strength and see what you're made of, with no other purpose than to challenge your limits and expose the depths of your soul. Then, there is the kind of training that develops you, reprograms you, and conditions you to perform at a higher level, for a *specific* purpose. Both types of training have their place, and quite often, advanced military training has slight elements of both types of training. Still, the training, or phases within, lean heavily toward one or the other – attempted destruction (testing/challenging) or development.

The Green Berets attend an initial "assessment and selection" that is a 19-day hell fest with no other purpose than to make each candidate fail. If the candidate passes this trying "selection" period, they proceed to the developmental (but still extremely tough) Qualification course, or "Q course". The first half aims to destroy and weed out anyone who isn't mentally or physically strong enough to survive the developmental phase and thrive in the ranks of fully fledged Special Forces soldiers. It challenges. That is its *only* goal. The second phase, the longer marathon, is where the warriors are truly made.

For Navy SEALs, the fabled BUDs training is storied for breaking some of the toughest men. However, that is not the only training SEALs must survive before being minted. BUDs is meant to challenge, and break. If the candidate passes BUDS, the SQT (SEAL Qualification Training) that follows is where SEALs learn the skills that make them gods of war.

The same structure, destruction then development, applies to countless other advanced military specializations and elite units within the military.

In my time in the military, we maintained a high standard of character and ethos by testing each other to the breaking point quite often, to see what we were each made of and ensure each of us still met the physical and mental standards needed to thrive in combat. This testing was essential. This "testing" assured we were tough enough and suitable for the challenges, tasks, and "development" that came next. The development, learning our respective crafts to the point of instinctive and highly accurate performance, nearly always happened in a separate "phase" than the initial and subsequent testing. That developmental phase was still always tough and not always formal training, with hundreds or thousands of hours of performance under our belts in a training environment. However, that developmental phase is always where the base habits and skills were ingrained.

The developmental phase, and training, is where we put in the work to win the battles to come and succeed in the operations to come.

Even at elite levels in the military, testing to see if you are strong enough to be developed, and instilling the skills, habits, and behaviors needed to excel were two different phases of training.

In the military, assessment, selection, and burst challenges are something to brag about – insanely difficult tasks and impressive accomplishments. Something wherein just finishing is an accomplishment, and actually "the" accomplishment. The only goal is completion.

However, the lasting positive effects of the challenge phase, beyond confidence, are nil. No new habits are programmed. No new skills are learned. The lasting skills, habits, and conditioning that make up "the elite" aren't formed there during that testing period.

Assessment, selection, and pure "challenges" test, but the habits that win battles, literally and figuratively in our daily lives, are deliberately trained to the level of instinct in the time of calm.

The development phase or the "pipeline" that follows is the process where lifelong warriors are conditioned, hardened, trained, and minted. The development that takes place is what makes them so effective in their operating environments, and in life.

In the 75 strong program, we are ingraining you with tools to win battles in daily life, instinctually and effortlessly. Completing matters, but building the habits matters more.

Herein lies the major difference between this program, 75 Strong, and the other popular 75-day challenge options: One tests while one develops

The popular 75-day challenge aims to test you. If you complete, you succeed. You win

The 75 strong program aims to develop you. These 75 days will instill instinctual practices, habits, and skills that empower your long-term mission – to be a stronger, better, more capable you. Every day.

Both structures – challenging and developing – have their place, and any well-lived life should have plenty of both

Now, you need to decide. Before you start *this* program, ask – are you after a finisher badge, or are you in this to build something long-term.

Do you want to prove that you're hard?

Or do you want to push how strong you can become?

If you simply want the test and a badge of finishing, with no assured long-term gains, and are more after the badge of finishing, the other popular 75-day challenges *may* be fine for you.

Consider jumping back to chapter 1 for some other "tests" I recommend that happen over a shorter period. Seventy-five days is a lot of time to invest just to see if you're tough enough. There are plenty of options for pushing your limits in 24 hours or less.

However...

If you want lasting positive change, our "75 Strong" program is what you need

We are taking the same approach to development as the best military training to "crawl, walk, run" our way to habits that put you on autopilot for your objective of living a fulfilling, healthy life.

If you've survived life to this point and have enough ambition to open this book, we'll assume you've passed "selection," and you're ready for your training course

Let's get started.

CHAPTER 7: WHAT NEXT?

We've completed 75 days straight of reinforcing beneficial habits to build a stronger you that will last far beyond 75 days.

Now, what?

First, sit back and take stock of what you've done and what you've accomplished. It likely hasn't been easy, and you've accomplished a lot more than a little bit, so take a moment to commend yourself and celebrate.

Next, sit back and think about each of the 10 daily tasks. How do you feel about each now? Which tasks felt worth the sacrifice? Which tasks felt lackluster and left you questioning their benefits?

Now, take stock of the results. How are your energy levels? What does your body feel like and look like now?

Last, decide which habits you will take into day 76 and beyond and which you will leave as successful accomplishments and that's all.

Going forward remember, do all things in moderation. You can bring a beer or a glass of wine back into your routine in moderation while maintaining the habit of being aware of what alcohol consumption costs you. You can reduce your workout days to 3 or 4 days a week while still committing to maintaining the habit of movement. You can compromise on your habits to achieve a level of moderation that makes the habits sustainable, enjoyable, and still beneficial.

Regardless of what you decide, I recommend maintaining as many of these habits and routines as possible because they are all possible and beneficial indefinitely.

Once you've decided the structure of your new habits, continue on with life as a stronger you, thanks to your stronger foundation.

Congratulations, and good luck on your newfound path.

ACKNOWLEDGMENTS

This book is the product of ideas and experiences I have gained from and with my families. This book is for them.

To my first family – Mom, Dad, Nacole, Casio, Adre, Jazmine, Evyan, Emory, Cameron, Caden, Dejesus, Brian, Octavia, Jeremy, Lenear – I wouldn't be the man I am today without the foundation you all carved and contributed to. Thank you.

To my second family – Matt, Alaina, Thomas, Lynden, Amelie, August, Di, Steve G., Dennis, Scott, Brett, all of Uncle Sam's Misguided Children, and every OIF and OEF vet out there – the situations I went through and survived with you all, have been some of the most trying and defining times of my life. I would not have survived them without you, and I wouldn't trade them for anything. Semper Fi.

To my third family, the pack of wanderers I've stumbled upon in the last four years – Alec, Arvin, Chris, Masha, Thoko, and Lex. I traveled the world to find paradise and ended up finding you guys. That says a lot. Thank you for sharing the adventure with me.

RESOURCES

For a list of the sources cited and a list of constantly updated resources, and link to a free printable journal, visit:

ABrotherAbroad.com/75-Strong-Resources

SOURCES

[1] Haddad, F., & Adams, G. R. (2002). Selected Contribution: Acute cellular and molecular responses to resistance exercise. Journal of Applied Physiology, 93(1), 394–403. https://doi.org/10.1152/japplphysiol.01153.2001

[2] Lally, Phillippa, et al. "How Are Habits Formed: Modelling Habit Formation in the Real World." European Journal of Social Psychology, vol. 40, no. 6, 2009, pp. 998–1009. Crossref, doi:10.1002/ejsp.674.

[3] Lally, Phillippa, et al. "How Are Habits Formed: Modelling Habit Formation in the Real World." European Journal of Social Psychology, vol. 40, no. 6, 2009, pp. 998–1009. Crossref, doi:10.1002/ejsp.674.

[4] McCullough, M. E., Emmons, R. A., & Tsang, J. A. (2002). The grateful disposition: A conceptual and empirical topography. Journal of Personality and Social Psychology, 82(1), 112–127. https://doi.org/10.1037/0022-3514.82.1.112

[5] Wong, Y. J., Owen, J., Gabana, N. T., Brown, J. W., McInnis, S., Toth, P., & Gilman, L. (2016). Does gratitude writing improve the mental health of psychotherapy clients? Evidence from a randomized controlled trial. Psychotherapy Research, 28(2), 192–202. https://doi.org/10.1080/10503307.2016.1169332

[6] Tod, D., Hardy, J., & Oliver, E. (2011). Effects of Self-Talk: A Systematic Review. Journal of Sport and Exercise Psychology, 33(5), 666–687. https://doi.org/10.1123/jsep.33.5.666

[7] Kross, E., Bruehlman-Senecal, E., Park, J., Burson, A., Dougherty, A., Shablack, H., Bremner, R., Moser, J., & Ayduk, O. (2014). Self-talk as a regulatory mechanism: How you do it matters. Journal of Personality and Social Psychology, 106(2), 304–324. https://doi.org/10.1037/a0035173

[8] Benabou, R., & Tirole, J. (2002). Self-Confidence and Personal Motivation. The Quarterly Journal of Economics, 117(3), 871–915. https://doi.org/10.1162/003355302760193913

[9] Desbordes, G., Negi, L. T., Pace, T. W. W., Wallace, B. A., Raison, C. L.,

& Schwartz, E. L. (2012). Effects of mindful-attention and compassion meditation training on amygdala response to emotional stimuli in an ordinary, non-meditative state. Frontiers in Human Neuroscience, 6. https://doi.org/10.3389/fnhum.2012.00292

[10] Bhasin, M. K., Denninger, J. W., Huffman, J. C., Joseph, M. G., Niles, H., Chad-Friedman, E., Goldman, R., Buczynski-Kelley, B., Mahoney, B. A., Fricchione, G. L., Dusek, J. A., Benson, H., Zusman, R. M., & Libermann, T. A. (2018). Specific Transcriptome Changes Associated with Blood Pressure Reduction in Hypertensive Patients After Relaxation Response Training. The Journal of Alternative and Complementary Medicine, 24(5), 486–504. https://doi.org/10.1089/acm.2017.0053

[11] Ekelund, U., Tarp, J., Steene-Johannessen, J., Hansen, B. H., Jefferis, B., Fagerland, M. W., Whincup, P., Diaz, K. M., Hooker, S. P., Chernofsky, A., Larson, M. G., Spartano, N., Vasan, R. S., Dohrn, I. M., Hagströmer, M., Edwardson, C., Yates, T., Shiroma, E., Anderssen, S. A., & Lee, I. M. (2019). Dose-response associations between accelerometry measured physical activity and sedentary time and all cause mortality: systematic review and harmonised meta-analysis. BMJ, l4570. https://doi.org/10.1136/bmj.l4570

[12] Chang Y. K., Etnier J. L. (2009). Exploring the dose-response relationship between resistance exercise intensity and cognitive function. J. Sport Exerc. Psychol. 31, 640–656. 10.1123/jsep.31.5.640

[13] Chang Y. K., Etnier J. L. (2009). Exploring the dose-response relationship between resistance exercise intensity and cognitive function. J. Sport Exerc. Psychol. 31, 640–656. 10.1123/jsep.31.5.640

[14] Monteiro, E. R. (2019, August 1). Effects of Different Between Test Rest Intervals in Reproducibility of the 10-Repetition Maximum Load Test: A Pilot Study with Recreationally Resistance Trained Men. PubMed. https://pubmed.ncbi.nlm.nih.gov/31523350/

[15] Walking: The Physical Activity Guidelines for Americans. (2020, September 17). Centers for Disease Control and Prevention. https://www.cdc.gov/physicalactivity/walking/index.htm

[16] Deborah Riebe, Jonathan K Ehrman, Gary Liguori, Meir Magal. Chapter 6 General Principles of Exercise Prescription. In: ACSM's Guidelines for Exercise Testing and Prescription. 10th Ed. Wolters Kluwer/Lippincott Williams & Wilkins, Philadelphia, PA: 2018, 143-179t

[17] Physical Activity Guidelines Advisory Committeepdf iconexternal icon [PDF-4.6MB]. Physical Activity Guidelines Advisory Committee Report, 2008. Washington, DC: U.S. Dept of Health and Human Services; 2008.

[18] Williamson, D. L., & Kirwan, J. P. (1997). A Single Bout of Concentric Resistance Exercise Increases Basal Metabolic Rate 48 Hours After

Exercise in Healthy 59–77-year-old Men. The Journals of Gerontology Series A: Biological Sciences and Medical Sciences, 52A(6), M352–M355. https://doi.org/10.1093/gerona/52a.6.m352

[19] Monteiro, E. R. (2019, August 1). Effects of Different Between Test Rest Intervals in Reproducibility of the 10-Repetition Maximum Load Test: A Pilot Study with Recreationally Resistance Trained Men. PubMed. https://pubmed.ncbi.nlm.nih.gov/31523350/

[20] Harvard Health. (2019, November 5). The sweet danger of sugar. https://www.health.harvard.edu/heart-health/the-sweet-danger-of-sugar

[21] Sutton, E. F., Beyl, R., Early, K. S., Cefalu, W. T., Ravussin, E., & Peterson, C. M. (2018). Early Time-Restricted Feeding Improves Insulin Sensitivity, Blood Pressure, and Oxidative Stress Even without Weight Loss in Men with Prediabetes. Cell Metabolism, 27(6), 1212–1221.e3. https://doi.org/10.1016/j.cmet.2018.04.010

[22] *Visit ABrotherAbroad.com/75-Strong-Resources to use the latest Basal Metabolic Rate calories calculator*

[23] Topiwala, A., Ebmeier, K. P., Maullin-Sapey, T., & Nichols, T. E. (2021). No safe level of alcohol consumption for brain health: observational cohort study of 25,378 UK Biobank participants. (Preprint). Published. https://doi.org/10.1101/2021.05.10.21256931

[24] O. Brien, C. P., & Lyons, F. (2000). Alcohol and the Athlete. Sports Medicine, 29(5), 295–300. https://doi.org/10.2165/00007256-200029050-00001

[25] World Health Organization. Global status report on alcohol and health 2018. Geneva, Switzerland. 2018.

[26] Kidd DC, Castano E. Reading literary fiction improves theory of mind. Science. 2013 Oct 18;342(6156):377-80. doi: 10.1126/science.1239918. Epub 2013 Oct 3. PMID: 24091705.

[27] Rizzolo, D., Zipp, G. P., Stiskal, D., & Simpkins, S. (2011). Stress Management Strategies For Students: The Immediate Effects Of Yoga, Humor, And Reading On Stress. Journal of College Teaching & Learning (TLC), 6(8). https://doi.org/10.19030/tlc.v6i8.1117

[28] Singer, L. M., & Alexander, P. A. (2016). Reading Across Mediums: Effects of Reading Digital and Print Texts on Comprehension and Calibration. The Journal of Experimental Education, 85(1), 155–172. https://doi.org/10.1080/00220973.2016.1143794

[29] Rogowsky, B. A., Calhoun, B. M., & Tallal, P. (2016). Does Modality Matter? The Effects of Reading, Listening, and Dual Modality on Comprehension. SAGE Open, 6(3), 215824401666955. https://doi.org/10.1177/2158244016669550

[30] Kidd DC, Castano E. Reading literary fiction improves theory of mind. Science. 2013 Oct 18;342(6156):377-80. doi: 10.1126/science.1239918. Epub 2013 Oct 3. PMID: 24091705.

[31] Rizzolo, D., Zipp, G. P., Stiskal, D., & Simpkins, S. (2011). Stress Management Strategies For Students: The Immediate Effects Of Yoga, Humor, And Reading On Stress. Journal of College Teaching & Learning (TLC), 6(8). https://doi.org/10.19030/tlc.v6i8.1117

[32] Singer, L. M., & Alexander, P. A. (2016). Reading Across Mediums: Effects of Reading Digital and Print Texts on Comprehension and Calibration. The Journal of Experimental Education, 85(1), 155–172. https://doi.org/10.1080/00220973.2016.1143794

[33] Vemuri, P., Lesnick, T. G., Przybelski, S. A., Machulda, M., Knopman, D. S., Mielke, M. M., Roberts, R. O., Geda, Y. E., Rocca, W. A., Petersen, R. C., & Jack, C. R. (2014). Association of Lifetime Intellectual Enrichment With Cognitive Decline in the Older Population. JAMA Neurology, 71(8), 1017. https://doi.org/10.1001/jamaneurol.2014.963

[34] Pressman, S. D., Matthews, K. A., Cohen, S., Martire, L. M., Scheier, M., Baum, A., & Schulz, R. (2009). Association of Enjoyable Leisure Activities With Psychological and Physical Well-Being. Psychosomatic Medicine, 71(7), 725–732. https://doi.org/10.1097/psy.0b013e3181ad7978

[35] Sio, U. N., & Ormerod, T. C. (2009). Does incubation enhance problem solving? A meta-analytic review. Psychological Bulletin, 135(1), 94–120. https://doi.org/10.1037/a0014212

[36] https://journals.sagepub.com/doi/10.1177/0956797612446024

[37] Taylor, Shelley E., Lien B. Pham, Inna D. Rivkin, and David A. Armor (1998), "Harnessing the
Imagination: Mental Simulation, Self-Regulation, and Coping," American Psychologist, 53 (4),
429-439.

[38] Zhao, Min, Steve Hoeffler, and Gal Zauberman (2005), "Mental Simulation and Preference
Consistency Over Time: The Role of Process- versus Outcome-Focused Thoughts," Working
Paper, University of North Carolina, Chapel Hill, NC 27599.

[39] Esterling, B. A., Antoni, M. H., Fletcher, M. A., Margulies, S., & Schneiderman, N. (1994). Emotional disclosure through writing or speaking modulates latent Epstein-Barr virus antibody titers. Journal of Consulting and Clinical Psychology, 62(1), 130–140. https://doi.org/10.1037/0022-006x.62.1.130

[40] Petrie, K. J., Booth, R. J., Pennebaker, J. W., Davison, K. P., & Thomas,

M. G. (1995). Disclosure of trauma and immune response to a hepatitis B vaccination program. Journal of Consulting and Clinical Psychology, 63(5), 787–792. https://doi.org/10.1037/0022-006x.63.5.787

Made in the USA
Monee, IL
01 October 2023